Navigating the Challenges
of
AI Testing

The Ultimate Professional's Guide to Mastering Solutions

Ilan Sezhiyan Jayaraman
Bidhu Ranjan Sahoo

Annu Roy

Navigating the Challenges of AI Testing
The Ultimate Professional's Guide to Mastering Solutions

Editor: Sowmya
Production Manager: Meghna and Alexa
Cover design by Freepik and Vecteezy
Formatting & Indexing: Gaurav Mutreja

First Edition: Nov-2024

Reference: 2308010

Published by Arcchie Publications

ISBN-13 (paperback): 978-81-974190-5-8
ISBN-13 (eBook): 978-81-974190-3-4

www.arcchieonline.com

DEDICATED TO

To those who have been my constant sources of inspiration and support. To my wife, Rekha, my unwavering rock, who believed in me even when I faltered. To my daughter, Lakshanya, whose love for learning mirrors my own. And to my parents, my guiding lights, whose encouragement has led me to a fulfilling career and life.

- Ilan Jayaraman

To my beloved wife Mina and our dear children, Ryansh and Samrat—your love and belief in me are the pillars of this journey. To my parents, Mr. K.C. Sahoo and Mrs. Minilata Sahoo, whose faith and blessings have shaped every step I take. This work is for you all, with all my love and gratitude.

- Bidhu Sahoo

My son Shikhar Srivastava, an ardent reader and budding writer.

- Annu Roy

FOREWORD

With over 26+ years of experience in the ever-evolving IT industry, I've had the privilege of spending most of my career in Quality Engineering, working alongside clients worldwide in diverse roles. Throughout my career, I've witnessed the remarkable transformation of QE & Test functions, with the pace of innovation accelerating exponentially in recent years. Over the last few years, my passion for AI has grown, and I'm convinced of its profound impact on the IT landscape. The advent of Generative AI has accelerated the adoption of AI across the IT landscape. There is practically no business process across any industry that is untouched by AI use cases which is pushing the envelope of driving more value for customers. Enterprises are seeing efficiencies across the entire range of processes ranging from Customer acquisition and support, Supply Chain efficiencies, Enterprise business process improvements, etc. So on one hand, we would have almost every IT system supporting every business function incorporating AI capabilities at a fast pace and at the same time we have rapid changes in the technology and its evolution, including its impact from diverse perspectives (such as legal, environmental, data, ethical, social etc.). This is a challenge as well as a great opportunity, specifically for QE organizations and professionals. It puts a tremendous onus on the QE functions in IT organizations to completely rethink their approach, methods, tools and mindset on ensuring quality of products and processes and assuring business users that their requirements would be met. For the first time, we are faced with probabilistic output rather than a deterministic output that we are so used to. At the same time, there is also the parallel thread of how to harness the power of AI to make QE & Test processes more efficient, driving quantum improvements for clients across the dimensions of cost, quality and time. It is obvious that the organizations and the professionals who get ahead of this new fundamental paradigm change in mindset and approach would have the greatest chance of success and growth. The book (Navigating the Challenges of AI Testing: A Journey to Technical Expert) provides a structured approach to the complexities and nuances of "QE of AI" and "AI in QE" .

This book explores the transformative intersection of Quality Engineering (QE) and Artificial Intelligence (AI), empowering readers to navigate the evolving QE landscape in the AI era. It begins with an introduction to AI fundamentals and their QE applications, followed by an examination of the paradigm shift towards probabilistic AI systems and necessary QE practice adaptations. The book then delves into AI system component evaluation, QE practice customization for effective AI testing, and QE enhancement through AI-driven approaches. Additionally, it covers generative AI's role in QE, AI-based testing and reporting methodologies, and essential skills for AI QE specialists. Finally, it provides a roadmap for becoming an AI testing thought leader, equipping readers with the knowledge, expertise, and vision to drive QE innovation and excellence. The details in the book have largely, if not entirely, come from the personal experiences and real-life learnings of the authors. That is what makes this book unique. It provides a perfect blend of more practical and realistic answers and solutions while guiding the reader on a step-by-step learning journey of an interesting yet challenging topic. It is a fascinating read, and a must read for someone wanting to go into the intricacies of the subject while at the same time wanting to use it in real life situations. It would, without a doubt, start your journey to be a thought leader.

Happy Reading!

Sandeep Mohapatra,
Practice Area Leader, IBM

ACKNOWLEDGMENT

Writing a book is a journey that extends far beyond the solitary act of putting words on paper. It is a deeply collaborative process, thriving on the inspiration, guidance, and support of others. As we reflect on the completion of this book, we are profoundly humbled and filled with gratitude for the countless individuals whose contributions have made this work possible.

First and foremost, we extend our heartfelt thanks to Mr. Sanal Menon, a seasoned thought leader in Quality Engineering Practice at IBM, for his expert advice and constructive criticism. His thoughtful insights and meticulous technical review have significantly enhanced the quality of this book, challenging us to think beyond our boundaries and pushing us to elevate our work to new heights. We are deeply grateful to the Arcchie Publications team—Mr. Vishesh Arora, Ms. Alexa E Adams, and Mr. Shambhu—whose dedication, enthusiasm, and unwavering commitment have been instrumental in bringing this book to life. Your expertise and tireless efforts have transformed our vision into reality, and for that, we are immensely thankful.

To our colleagues and peers who generously offered their insights and feedback, we extend our deepest appreciation. Your thoughtful contributions have enriched the content and depth of this book, leaving a lasting impression on its pages.

We are also indebted to our families for their enduring patience, understanding, and support throughout the long hours spent on this book. Special thanks go to Mrs. Rekha Krishnan, Miss Lakshanya Ilan, Mrs. Minarani Palei, Master Ryansh Sahoo, Master Samrat Bidhu Sahoo, Mr. Shikar Srivastava, and Mr. Sachin Srivastava—your encouragement and belief in us were the driving forces that kept us going through the most challenging times.

To our parents, friends, and loved ones, we owe a special debt of gratitude. Your enduring patience, understanding, and encouragement during the countless hours we spent immersed in research and writing have been the cornerstone of this journey. Your unwavering support has been invaluable, and we are forever grateful. Finally, our gratitude extends to the readers—both novice and expert—who will embark on this exploration with us. It is our sincere hope that this book ignites your curiosity, expands your knowledge, and inspires you to push the boundaries of technological wisdom.

Thank you all for being an integral part of this journey.

- Ilan Jayaraman, Bidhu Sahoo & Annu Roy

ABOUT THE AUTHORS

- **Ilan Sezhiyan Jayaraman** is a certified Thought Leader on quality engineering with extensive experience in AI testing. He has led the development of the IBM Quality Platform and AI Testing Offering for IBM, and has driven critical initiatives, including the development of patented IBM Research assets. With a strong foundation of core technical and architectural capabilities, Ilan brings a unique blend of technical expertise, business acumen, and collaboration skills to his work. He has worked closely with clients and delivery teams in a consultant capacity, helping them transform their quality engineering practices. His expertise spans AI testing, mainframe modernization, and data-based modernization, among other areas. His ability to bridge the gap between technology and business has enabled him to deliver innovative solutions that meet client needs.

- **Bidhu Ranjan Sahoo** is a seasoned Enterprise Test Architect and Innovator with over two decades of experience in quality engineering. As the IBM Service Area Leader for Hybrid Cloud, Middleware, and Network Cloudification in Quality Engineering practice, he is overseeing global client support and managing practices of 1000+ resources. He has extensive experience in digital and hybrid cloud test solutions and deliveries for various enterprise clients. Bidhu has co-authored 10 patents in Blockchain, Security, Microservices, DevOps and Testing. His expertise in hyper-scalars like AWS, Azure, IBM Cloud, and Red Hat OpenShift has enabled him to deliver innovative solutions that meet client needs. He aims to provide insightful perspectives, practical guidance, and innovative approaches for leveraging AI in ensuring software quality.

- **Annu Roy** is a Service Area Leader managing and collaborating with a team of technical experts to help clients adopt modern ways of working in their IT landscape. She is a PMP certified, senior Program Manager with experience in Complex Program Management. She has led diverse and distributed, multi-disciplinary teams of Application Leads, Architects, Business Analysts and technical resources located in different geographies, spanning Government, Healthcare and Finance industries. She is a certified Scrum Master, SAFe Agilist and ITIL V3 Expert. She has more than 2 decades of experience in the IT Industry working with multiple big brands. She has a passion for mentoring students and professionals and believes that every individual deserves an opportunity to learn and grow.

ABOUT THE TECHNICAL REVIEWERS

- **Sanal Menon** is a Quality Engineering Thought Leader with global experience in providing leadership to IT Services Delivery, Consulting and Sales. He is known in his circle as a critical thinker who has architected Test Transformation solutions, Capability models with a view of futuristic and evolving technological landscape. As a Peoples Person, he has mentored, coached and developed people to help them stay ahead of the dynamic delivery models and disruptive technologies, with a strong proponent of the quote "You are as good as your last delivery!".

- **Dr Gaurav Arora** is a Microsoft MVP award recipient. He is a Mentor of Change with AIM NITI Aayog, Govt. of India, Business Coach with Business Blaster, Govt of NCT of Delhi. He is a lifetime member of the Computer Society of India (CSI), an advisory member and senior mentor at IndiaMentor, certified as a Scrum trainer and coach, ITIL-F certified, and PRINCE-F and PRINCE-P certified. Gaurav is an open-source developer and a contributor to the Microsoft TechNet community. He has authored books across-the-technologies. Recently, Gaurav has recognized as a world record holder for writing books in exceptional technologies..

PREFACE

As we navigate the complexities of the digital age, the role of quality engineering is evolving at an unprecedented pace. With the increasing adoption of artificial intelligence (AI) and machine learning (ML) across various industries, the demand for quality engineers capable of testing and validating these systems is growing exponentially. In this book, we examine the challenges and opportunities that AI and ML present for quality engineers. We explore the paradigm shift in quality engineering, where traditional testing methods and tools are no longer sufficient to ensure the reliability and performance of AI-driven applications.

Combining theoretical foundations with practical applications, this book serves as a comprehensive guide to addressing the challenges of AI testing. It delves into the fundamentals of AI and ML while highlighting the pivotal role of quality engineers in ensuring the reliability and performance of AI-infused systems. Real-world examples and case studies are woven throughout the book to illustrate the challenges and opportunities AI and ML create for quality engineers. Practical solutions and best practices are provided to address these challenges, along with an exploration of the future of quality engineering in the age of AI and ML.

This book is designed for quality engineers, software developers, and anyone interested in ensuring the quality and reliability of AI-infused applications. Whether you are a seasoned professional or new to the field, this resource equips you with the knowledge and skills needed to navigate the complexities of AI testing and drive the success of your projects.

Let's embark on this journey of learning together.

What's Inside This Book

Chapter 1: Introduction to Quality Engineering in the Era of AI provides an overview of the evolution of quality engineering and its growing significance in today's technology landscape. It highlights the expanding role of quality engineers beyond traditional testing, emphasizing the importance of quality evaluation throughout the product lifecycle. The chapter also examines the transformative impact of AI on quality engineering, showcasing its potential to revolutionize the field.

Chapter 2: Fundamentals of AI for Quality Engineers introduces the foundational concepts of AI and its diverse applications. It explores AI's role in optimizing and automating quality engineering processes, discussing both the advantages and challenges of integrating AI into these practices. Key AI terminology and concepts are explained to equip quality engineers with a solid knowledge base for further exploration.

Chapter 3: Paradigm Shift: Evaluating Probabilistic AI Systems contrasts deterministic and probabilistic AI systems, emphasizing the unique challenges of evaluating probabilistic systems. It provides guidance on adapting quality engineering practices to assess the reliability and performance of such systems, incorporating statistical analysis techniques for evaluating probabilistic outputs.

Chapter 4: Evaluating Components of AI Systems examines the various components of AI systems, including machine learning models, data pipelines, and algorithms. It outlines quality evaluation methods for each component, offering strategies for identifying and addressing quality issues. The importance of understanding the interactions among AI system components is also discussed.

Chapter 5: Customizing QE Practices for AI focuses on adapting traditional quality engineering practices for AI systems. It highlights the importance of defining AI-specific quality metrics and objectives, introduces AI-specific testing techniques such as model validation and data quality assessment, and provides guidance on ensuring regulatory compliance in AI-driven solutions.

Chapter 6: Leveraging AI to Enhance QE Practices explores the use of AI to optimize quality engineering activities. It discusses the benefits and challenges of adopting AI in quality engineering, introduces AI-based tools and frameworks, and provides practical insights on using AI for test case generation, test data creation, and defect prediction.

Chapter 7: Generative AI and Its Role in QE delves into generative AI and its implications for quality engineering. It addresses ethical considerations and challenges associated with generative AI, offering guidance on utilizing these techniques for diverse and effective test case generation.

Chapter 8: AI-Based Application Testing and Reporting introduces advanced AI-based testing approaches, emphasizing the use of AI for intelligent test execution and prioritization. It provides strategies for effectively reporting and communicating AI-driven evaluation results at each phase of the delivery lifecycle. Best practices for documenting and presenting AI testing outcomes are also covered.

For Whom This Book Is Intended

This book is designed for:

- Quality engineering professionals aiming to enhance their skills in testing AI-driven applications.

- Software engineers, architects, and project managers collaborating with quality engineers to deliver defect-free products through modern development lifecycles.

- Professionals seeking to transition into AI testing or quality engineering.

- Individuals interested in understanding the challenges and opportunities of AI testing..

Download the source code and colored images:

To download the source code bundle

and the colored images, please follow the link

OR

scan the QR Code

https://l1nq.com/9788197419058

Errata

At **ARCCHIE Publications**, we are committed to delivering the highest-quality content in all our publications. We follow best practices to ensure the accuracy of our content to provide our readers with an indulgent reading experience. We believe and understand that our readers are our best judges, and we always use their input and feedback from time to time to improve human errors, if any, that may occur during the publishing processes involved. We invite you to participate in our errata submission process to ensure our books remain accurate and up to date. Please help us reach out to readers who might have difficulties due to unforeseen errors. Please write to us at *errata@arcchieonline.com*.

When submitting errata, please include the following information:

- Book Title
- Reference#
- Author(s)
- Page Number
- Description of the Error
- Suggested Correction (if applicable)

The **ARCCHIE Publications** Family highly appreciates your support, suggestions, and feedback.

Sharing Your Perspective and Providing Feedback

Your perspective is invaluable to us, as it helps us enhance our content and gather your feedback. We warmly welcome all forms of feedback. Please feel free to send us an email at **feedback@arcchieonline.com**, mentioning the book title in the subject line of your message.

Book Review Invitation

We kindly invite you to share your thoughts. After you've read and engaged with this book, consider leaving a review on the platform where you acquired it. Your impartial feedback can greatly assist potential readers in making informed decisions. Your reviews provide valuable insights for us at **Arcchie**, helping us better understand your perspectives on our products, and they offer authors the chance to appreciate your feedback on their work.

PIRACY

Should you encounter unauthorized reproductions of our publications in any digital format on the internet, we kindly request your assistance in pinpointing their locations or website sources. Please reach out to us at **copyright@arcchieonline.com** and include a link to the infringing material.

If you possess expertise in a particular subject and wish to participate in the creation or contribution to a book, please visit *authors.arcchieonline.com*. We welcome you and assist you to start your authorship journey with **ARCCHIE PUBLICATIONS**.

TABLE OF CONTENTS

Chapter 1

Quality Engineering in the Era of AI

The realm of Quality Engineering (QE) is committed to maintaining the excellence and reliability of products and processes throughout their entire development lifecycle. This involves application of engineering principles, methodologies, and practices to establish, execute, and maintain quality control systems. In this chapter, we will delve into the impact of artificial intelligence (AI) on QE processes and it's role in shaping and revolutionizing this domain.

In this chapter, we will discuss the following topics:

- Evolution of Quality Engineering and its significance in the current technology era
- Quality Engineering processes encompass several key activities that play vital roles in ensuring high-quality outcomes
- Expanding the role of quality engineers beyond testing
- The Evolving Role of Quality Engineers in the Changing Landscape of Software Testing
- AI and Quality Engineering: Embracing the Power of Artificial Intelligence
- AI and Quality Engineering can be approached in two distinct contexts

Evolution of quality engineering and its significance in the current technology era

Over the last several decades, we have lived through evolutions in the IT industry in the areas of technology, delivery methods, practices, metrics, measurements and KPI's. To recall, there is no one area which can be claimed as not affected by the changes or evolutions over time.

Quality Assurance (QA), Quality Control (QC) and Testing, Processes, Defect Detection and Defect Prevention, Delivered Defect Density etc.; all these were the core concepts that defined quality. If all these metrics in the Quality life were controlled, the quality of the product would be deemed acceptable. We had process reviews to control process quality and gating checks to control product quality.

While these checks were necessary to ensure overall quality of the product, they were more focused on defect detection. This, as a mindset, implied that defects will be detected after the fact or after an event has occurred.

To put this into perspective:

- Application developers develop the code, complete unit test.

- If an iterative development model is adopted, the application code is passed on to the tester. The testing uncovers defects or bugs, which is again passed back to the developer (Note: In a waterfall model, the testers get to find defect after the whole application module is completed).

- The defects are fixed and sent back to the tester to re-test. This process continues.

- Metrics on number of defects "Detected" in the testing phase often were cited as a measure of quality.

- These metrics had a subjective element to it, meaning, they either made the Tester look good and a Developer look bad (or vice versa). While these were not deliberated, the whole process and mindset of Quality brought them into the system. This often was countering the "Collaborative" team concept.

We have evolved from this model to a Quality Engineering (QE) model in recent years, driven by the ever-changing IT landscape and the increasing demand for a more comprehensive approach in evaluating product quality. Given the focus on speed to market, there is higher interest for more frequent and incremental releases of the product features into production. This has influenced the need for changes to the application Quality is perceived. Businesses are no longer satisfied with mere testing; they now expect a holistic perspective that encompasses various activities to prevent defects, optimize processes, and improve overall quality.

The fundamental difference between QE and Testing is that testing focuses on unearthing defects through evaluating the testable product or application. The gating processes which happen at the end of a phase "Detects" defects. In contrast, QE focuses on preventing defects from cascading to the subsequent phases of the solution development life cycle. This whole shift from "Defect Detection" to "Defect Prevention" requires significant change to the mindset of Quality. While testing primarily revolves around uncovering defects through evaluating the testable product or application, QE takes a proactive stance, emphasizing defect prevention throughout the entire solution development life cycle. This distinction is crucial in meeting the evolving needs of the technology industry and project delivery methods.

The rapid advancement of technology, including Artificial Intelligence (AI), Internet of Things (IoT), Cloud computing, and big data, have introduced new complexities and challenges to the quality evaluation process. The traditional approach of testing the product before its delivery is reactive, only to validate the quality retrospectively. To improve the efficiency of the quality assurance process, a proactive approach is necessary, one that evaluates every stage of product development from concept or inception phase. This approach ensures that quality is ingrained into every aspect of the product, from its initial design to its final implementation. To fulfill this demand, a combination of engineering practices, technology and automation is delivered through the framework of Quality Engineering. Refer **Fig 1.1** depicting '360⁰ View of Quality Engineering'.

Figure 1.1: *360⁰ View of Quality Engineering*

Consider an example of a Quality Engineer aspiring to excel in testing AI-based IoT solutions, it's crucial to recognize the evolving landscape of technology and the shift in mindset required to effectively test Internet of Things (IoT) applications. Transitioning from traditional testing to AI-based IoT testing involves thinking holistically about the system, considering both software and hardware, and embracing a more integrated approach. For IoT applications, which are often embedded in appliances like washing machines, televisions, commercial manufacturing robots, and car head units, a robust simulation environment is essential for comprehensive pre-deployment testing. This approach includes validating the embedded user interface, integration layers (API Layer), and backend systems. Quality Engineers must develop versatile skills in UI, middleware, and backend testing, employing industry practices such as automated testing, CI/CD pipelines, security testing, and performance testing to enhance the process. By adopting this comprehensive and integrated approach, continuously updating skills, and incorporating industry best practices, Quality Engineers can ensure the delivery of high-quality, reliable, and secure IoT applications.

Quality Planning

Quality planning is the first aspect of quality engineering processes. It involves defining a product or service's quality standards, objectives, and metrics. It involves identifying customer requirements, setting quality goals, and developing a plan to achieve them efficiently.

Quality planning helps meet stakeholder expectations, define the project's scope and success criteria, and evaluate and allocate the necessary resources and tools. It also helps to identify and mitigate any potential risks that could affect the quality of the product or service.

For example, in a software product development project, quality planning may include activities such as:

- Conducting market research and user surveys to understand the needs and preferences of the target customers

- Defining the functional and non-functional requirements of the software product

- Developing a quality management plan that specifies the quality standards, objectives, metrics, roles, responsibilities, and activities for the project

- Selecting the appropriate methodologies, frameworks, tools, and techniques for software development and testing

- Performing a risk analysis to identify and prioritize the potential sources of defects, errors, or failure points in the software product or service.

Building upon the foundation of quality planning, quality assurance ensures that products or services meet defined quality standards through a structured and systematic set of evaluation processes. It aims to prevent defects, errors, or failures, and encourages a culture of continuous improvement within the organization.

Quality Assurance

Quality assurance is the second aspect of quality engineering processes. It ensures that products or services meet defined quality standards through a structured and systematic set of processes for evaluation. Commonly used processes like inspections, audits, and reviews are conducted to identify and address any deviations from expectations set on the quality of the deliverables.

The primary objective of Quality assurance is to prevent defects, errors, or failures from occurring. It should also ensure compliance with regulations and standards. It encourages the organization to build a quality culture by promoting best practices and continuous improvement.

For example, in software development, quality assurance may include quality checks such as:

- The definition of the overall test strategy includes test objectives, scope, and test coverage. It defines the necessary infrastructure, tools, timelines, and resources.

- Test cases are developed to evaluate each component of the software, based on the functional specifications and behavior. These test cases are derived from the defined requirements and functional specifications.

- Defects are identified by evaluating the outcomes of test case executions. These defects or bugs indicate non-compliance of the software's behavior with the expected outcomes.

- The quality assurance activities and metrics are documented to assess the efficiency of the developed software against the requirements and functional specifications.

- Training and coaching are provided to the testing staff to enhance their quality awareness, skills and capabilities.

Quality control proactively monitors and verifies the quality of products or processes during implementation. By detecting and resolving problems at the earliest stage, quality control promotes continuous improvement and data-driven decision-making.

Quality Control

Quality control is the third aspect of quality engineering processes. While Quality Assurance focuses on testing the products or processes in the testing phase, Quality Control focuses on monitoring and verifying the quality of products or processes during production or implementation. Inspection, measurement, and controlling of defects or non-conformities are performed in this activity.

Quality control is a proactive approach to detect and resolve problems at the earliest stage possible. It includes monitoring and controlling through feedback and data for quality improvement initiatives.

For example, in software development, quality control may include activities such as:

- Evaluating the ticket trends and ensuring preventive actions are taken to reduce production tickets. Ticket Management is a significant task performed as part of Quality Control.

- Production system performance and monitoring to detect bottlenecks, evaluate system performance through system logs analysis, and take corrective actions to resolve them.

- Regularly analyze system logs to identify possible data issues and take corrective actions to resolve them. Based on historical patterns analysis of the logs, proactive steps can be taken to prevent issues.

Complementing quality control efforts, statistical analysis in quality engineering uses various methods and tools to analyze data, identify trends and patterns, and facilitate data-driven decision-making. It helps measure and evaluate performance, identify optimization opportunities, and support quality improvement initiatives.

Statistical Analysis

Statistical analysis is the fourth aspect of quality engineering processes. It utilizes statistical methods and tools to analyze data and enable data-driven decision-making. This approach assists in identifying trends, patterns, and root causes of quality issues, thereby facilitating process improvements.

Statistical analysis helps to measure and evaluate the performance of products or processes, identify opportunities for optimization, and support quality improvement initiatives. It also helps to provide evidence and justification for any changes or actions taken.

For example, in software development, statistical analysis may include activities such as:

- Production log analysis to provide insights into data patterns and system behavior analysis to predict the occurrences of issues, thereby enabling preventive actions.

- Applying descriptive and inferential statistics to summarize and compare defects data, such as mean, median, mode, standard deviation, confidence interval, hypothesis testing, and so on, can help take a defect preventive approach.

- Production system performance assessed using graphical tools such as histograms, box plots, scatter plots, control charts to visualize and interpret data such as distribution, variation, correlation, trend, bottleneck, etc., and take action to resolve the issues.

- Reporting and presenting data analysis results and recommendations using tables, charts, graphs, etc.

To effectively measure and track the performance of quality engineering processes, the some of the following KPIs can be adopted:

- Defect Density: Measures the number of defects per unit size of the software, helping in identifying areas that need improvement.

- Test Coverage: The percentage of the applications covered by tests, indicating the thoroughness of the testing process.

- Customer Found Defects (CFD): The number of defects found by customers after release, reflecting the quality of the product delivered.

Building on the insights gained through statistical analysis, continuous improvement is a fundamental aspect of quality engineering processes, promoting a culture of constantly improving systems, processes and services. By adapting to changing customer needs and expectations, continuous improvement contributes to increased efficiency, productivity, profitability and customer satisfaction.

Continuous Improvement

Continuous improvement is the fifth aspect of quality engineering processes. In the current era of QE, continuous improvement is a hygiene factor, meaning, a culture to adopt an approach to continuously improve the QE processes is expected by every client and is not an option. This process involves continuously monitoring systems under QE and taking proactive steps to improve the system's efficiency, processes and services.

Continuous improvement helps to maintain and improve the quality level of products or services over time, to adapt to changing customer needs and expectations, and to achieve excellence. It also helps to increase efficiency, productivity, profitability, and customer satisfaction.

For example, in software development, continuous improvement may include activities such as:

- **Collaborating with Development Teams**: Engaging with development teams during sprint planning ensures testing requirements are considered. This collaboration helps identify and prioritize testable components.

- **Defining Clear Acceptance Criteria**: Establishing clear acceptance criteria for user stories ensures they are testable. This includes specifying the conditions under which a user stories ensures they are testable. This includes specifying the conditions under which a user story is considered complete.

- **Integrating Test Automation**: Incorporating test automation early in the sprint cycle enables continuous testing. Automated tests can be run frequently to catch issues early and ensure new code changes do not introduce new defects.

- **Mock Services and Simulators**: Using mock services and simulators creates a virtual environment that mimics the actual system. This enables testing components in isolation and ensures integration points are validated.

- **Continuous Integration/Continuous Deployment (CI/CD)**: Implementing Continuous testing method in CI/CD pipelines to automate the build, test, and deployment processes. This ensures code changes are continuously integrated and tested, even without the complete system.

- **Automated Testing**: Enhancing automated testing frameworks to cover more scenarios reduces manual testing efforts, increases test coverage, and accelerates feedback loops.

- **Infrastructure as Code (IaC)**: Adopting IaC practices automates infrastructure provisioning and management, ensuring consistency and reducing the risk of configuration drift.

- **Monitoring and Feedback Loops**: Implementing robust monitoring and feedback mechanisms tracks system performance and user behavior. This data can be used to make informed decisions and drive improvements.

- **Cross-Functional Teams**: Encouraging cross-functional teams that include developers, testers, and operations personnel promotes collaboration and ensures quality is a shared responsibility.

As a culmination of previous quality engineering aspects, risk management focuses on identifying, analyzing, and mitigating potential risks that could impact product quality. By protecting product quality from internal and external threats, risk management helps increase customer satisfaction, reduce uncertainty and ensure compliance with legal and ethical obligations.

Risk Management

Risk management is the sixth aspect of quality engineering processes. Every project or process delivery includes Risk Management. It assesses and mitigates risks that could impact product quality by identifying potential risks, analyzing their impact and developing strategies to minimize the impact or eliminate them.

Risk management helps to protect product quality from internal or external threats to reduce uncertainty and variability, and to increase customer satisfaction and confidence. It also helps to comply with legal and ethical obligations and responsibilities.

For example, in software development, risk management may include activities such as:

- Risk assessment during the contracting process to evaluate potential risks like the availability of data, skills, infrastructure and cost perspective to identify their probability of occurrence and impact, as early as possible.

- Developing a risk management plan specifying risk mitigation strategy such as avoidance, reduction, transfer or acceptance for each risk.

- Identify risk mitigation strategies such as design reviews, testing, verification, validation, backup systems, contingency plans, insurance policies, etc.

- Monitor and review the risk status and performance indicators such as risk probability, impact, exposure, severity, etc.

- Update and revise the risk assessment and management plan as needed based on the changes in the product or service requirements, environment, or stakeholder expectations.

These key factors influence the overall quality of delivery of the organization and enable a culture of quality. Let us now understand the critical activities in QE processes.

Quality Engineering processes encompass several key activities that play vital roles in ensuring high-quality outcomes

To ensure optimal quality outcomes in products and services, the Quality Engineering life cycle consists of several essential stages, including requirement analysis and planning, design, testing, test results analysis and reporting, and maintenance. Each stage plays a crucial role in comprehending the application, formulating test strategies, executing tests, analyzing results, and maintaining artifacts for continuous improvement.

- **Requirement Analysis and Planning**: This activity involves a comprehensive understanding of the application or product, considering its technology, functionality, performance, infrastructure and domain perspectives. The scope is defined, and a test strategy is formulated, outlining how the application or product will be tested.

- **Design**: Developing a test design approach is essential to ensure sufficient coverage of all changes or modules. The test design should adopt a structured approach to test applications, covering all the impacted changes. The testing methodology, including the choice between manual versus automated testing, is determined in this phase.

- **Testing**: The execution of test cases and the evaluation of test results against the defined requirements occur in this stage. It aims to validate compliance, identify potential issues or deviations from expected outcomes and report them.

- **Test Results Analysis and Reporting**: An analysis of the test results is performed to identify areas of strength and weakness throughout the previous stages of the life cycle. This analysis allows for identifying the root causes behind issues or weaknesses in the process. Recommendations are provided to improve the process, methods and tooling (PMT) within the delivery life cycle to prevent defects from propagating into subsequent QE phases and cycles.

- **Maintenance**: All QE artifacts developed and documented throughout the QE life cycle must be maintained for future releases. Recommendations for improving the PMT should be executed to enhance the overall QE capability of the delivery organization.

By embracing Quality Engineering practices, organizations can optimize processes, prevent defects, and improve overall product quality in today's technology-driven era. Integrating QE methodologies with the latest technological advancements ensures that quality is a focal point throughout the product development life cycle, leading to more efficient and reliable solutions that meet the ever-increasing demands of clients and users.

Expanding the role of quality engineers beyond testing

We will delve into the role of testers and their significance in the software development landscape a decade or so ago. Back then, the responsibilities of quality engineering were primarily focused on testing the product. Testers were crucial in evaluating adherence to requirements, uncovering defects and ensuring quality. However, the industry dynamics have shifted, leading to changes in the perception and demands placed on testers. In subsequent chapters, we will explore the impact of AI adoption on this evolving role. However, first, let us examine the key points that defined the role of testers.

Evaluating Adherence to Requirements: Testers were primarily responsible for evaluating the product or service's compliance with specified requirements. Their expertise in understanding and interpreting requirements was critical in ensuring that the product met the intended goals.

Unearthing Defects: Testers were tasked with identifying and reporting as many defects as possible in the test environment. This involved executing numerous test cases to thoroughly examine the product's functionality, performance, and usability—their meticulous efforts aimed at improving the overall quality of the software or service.

Late Involvement in Waterfall Delivery: In the traditional waterfall delivery method, testers' involvement typically occurs in the final stages of the software development life cycle. Many a times, the level of testing was reduced or ignored due to the pressure to release the product into UAT. Consequently, defects that went unnoticed during testing would surface in the UAT and/or production environments.

Perception of Quality in Agile: With the advent of agile delivery processes, some clients perceived quality standards to be more flexible. In some instances, the identified issues were moved to the backlog and scheduled for subsequent releases. This approach seemingly diminished the significance of the tester's role, rendering it redundant or trivial. However, over time, this approach was proven counterproductive in various industries, leading clients to demand the integration of testers as part of agile delivery squads. Researchers and analysts widely agree on the importance of testers in agile methodologies.

Manual Testing and Automation: A decade ago, manual testing was generally deemed acceptable and sufficient for fulfilling the role of a tester. Automation of test case execution was considered a specialized and niche skill, requiring a dedicated team of subject matter experts (SMEs) to develop the automation framework. Automation was gradually gaining recognition but had yet to become a widespread practice.

Domain Knowledge and Technical Expertise: Testers were expected to possess sound knowledge of the application domain, such as banking, retail, pharmaceuticals, etc. However, in many client engagements, limited technical knowledge was considered acceptable. Testers primarily focused on their domain expertise, while technical skills were not a primary requirement.

The role of testers a decade ago was centered around evaluating adherence to requirements, uncovering defects, and ensuring quality. With the advent of agile methodologies, the perception of quality and the role of testers changed. While manual testing sufficed at the time, the importance of automation, to align with the expectations of speed to market and consistency in quality, were gradually recognized. Furthermore, testers were expected to have domain knowledge, with limited emphasis on technical expertise. In subsequent chapters, we will explore how the role of testers has evolved in the context of AI adoption.

The Evolving Role of Quality Engineers in the Changing Landscape of Software Testing

Having established the need for change in the role of a tester, Quality Engineering approach brought the necessary need to enhance the role of Quality Engineer. The nature of quality engineering approach needs a paradigm shift in the mind-set of how quality engineering as a role is perceived, thereby directly impacting the skills needed to perform the role of a Quality Engineer.

Let us explore the changing role of testers and the emergence of quality engineering skills. We will discuss the need for a shift in mind-set for the role, the responsibilities of quality engineers and the overlapping skills with developers. Furthermore, we will delve into the importance of multi-dimensional testing skills and the growing demand for automation in quality engineering practices.

The Role of a Quality Engineer in Agile Delivery

The Role of a Quality Engineer in Agile Delivery: Quality Engineers play a vital role in ensuring the highest level of quality throughout the Agile delivery process. As gatekeepers at every phase in a sprint, they actively evaluate deliverables, validate requirements, assess design phases, develop automated test case design and execution, evaluate unit-tested code, generate automated test reports and maintain adaptability in response to changing requirements (**Fig.1.2**).

Figure 1.2: *Role of a Quality Engineer in AI Testing*

You will learn these in more details in following:

Test Strategy and Planning

In an Agile delivery framework, a quality engineer should prepare the end-to-end test strategy and plan.

Test Strategy and Planning includes:

- Defining the scope of each Agile sprint, including the specific features and functionalities to be tested.

- Determining the types of testing needed, such as Unit Testing, Functional Testing, Non-Functional Testing, or technology-specific testing.

- Identifying the Test scenarios based on requirements and scope.

- Determining the Test Data needed for test execution, including any preconditions.

- Identification of automation potential for the current sprint to improve efficiency and effectiveness.

- Selecting a Defect Management solution to track and manage issues discovered during testing.

Validate Requirements

Quality engineers should validate the quality of the requirements in the scope of Agile Sprint. Some of the key aspects of validating requirements are:

- Ensuring clarity in the Requirements by avoiding ambiguous statements that could result in scope creep.

- Identifying impacted applications or business functions that need to be tested to ensure comprehensive coverage.

- Assessing the complexity of the requirement to prioritize and sequence test execution for optimal efficiency.

- Identifying dependent requirements for test execution sequencing to avoid potential blockers.

Design the Test Cases

During the design phase, quality engineers should consider the following activities:

- Deciding between reusing existing test cases and developing new test cases based on the requirements and scope.

- Determining if test data provisioning and generation is needed to support testing efforts.

- Evaluating test coverage to ensure all aspects of the application are thoroughly tested.

- Ensuring traceability of changes to support effective testing and issue resolution.

- Automating test design using mathematical approaches Combinatorial

Test Design (CTD) and AI approaches like generating test cases using Generative AI.

Design Test Case Execution Automation

In the Agile delivery model, the sprint duration can range from 2-4 weeks. Quality engineers are expected to test the sprint deliverables in a short duration. To support this, automated test case execution plays a significant role. Some of the key expectations are:

- Developing test automation scripts to execute the test cases for the current sprint, not for subsequent sprints. To accomplish this, an appropriate test automation strategy should be adopted.
- Ensuring Test Automation scripts are developed and tested before executing the test case to avoid delays and errors.

Performance Testing

Quality engineers need to execute the test cases in the scope of the sprint. They need to perform the following activities:

- Executing automated test cases to improve efficiency and reduce manual effort.
- Capturing Test Results to support analysis and reporting.

Validate and Report Test Outcome

Quality engineers need to validate and report the test outcome. Key tasks in this phase are:

- Validating the test results, marking them as a pass or fail based on the outcome and documenting any issues discovered.
- Raising defects for the failed test cases to support issue resolution.
- Generating Test Reports to communicate testing progress and results to stakeholders.

Overlapping Skills of Testers and Developers in Quality Engineering

Overlapping skills does not imply that developers and quality engineers will interchange roles. While there are small number of roles where Application

Developers double hat as Quality Engineers in a capacity to apply maintenance fixes to application code, in all other application development, Quality Engineers have a distinct role. Overlapping is more in the sense that unlike in the past, Quality Engineers now bring in technology angle to effectively apply quality in the entire product development lifecycle. It requires a more comprehensive approach than traditional software testing. It fosters increased collaboration between testers and developers by way of driving development based on "What" and "How" a feature can be tested (example: -A Test Driven Development approach). This synergy allows for shared responsibilities and a stronger commitment to delivering software quality.

Holistic Approach to Quality Engineering

Quality Engineers take a holistic approach by participating in defining quality standards, establishing quality assurance processes, conducting risk assessments and implementing continuous improvement initiatives. To effectively apply QE practices, Quality Engineers must understand the underlying technology used in product development. Automating time consuming processes, activities and product testing require strong programming skills to build automation frameworks that seamlessly integrate with various components of the product or application. They must thoroughly understand emerging technologies to help them choose the right automation tools and to adopt end to end automation of the application and its components.

The Need for Multi-Dimensional Testing Skills

Advancement in technology brings with it underlying complexities in the software development environment. Quality Engineers must stay at par with these advancements by acquiring a wide range of skills and expertise. From a Quality Engineering paradigm, we have moved away from the traditional siloed skill categorization. For example, in the traditional world, we had pockets of specialization such as Functional Testers, Automation Testers, Mobile Testers etc. In the new world, applications are going the Omnichannel way and deployed on multiple digital platforms.

Any e-commerce or social media platforms today are available as a portal and on a mobile as an app. They are integrated with different internal or external application systems or COTS using API's. Data Engineering and analytics are used by these systems to make real time decisions to offer products to customers. The application development and delivery models have transformed from waterfall and iterative to Agile and squad-based models. Let's look at this scenario practically. Assume you are working in an Agile squad of 8 members. You cannot have 50% of them as testers having skills in Functional, Mobile, Microservices and Automation. This fails the construct of a squad-based delivery model, impacting cost, schedule and speed to market. The expectation is for a Quality Engineer to have skills to test across all the digital platforms. With technological advancements, quality engineers need to possess multi-dimensional testing skills. For instance, testing a mobile application requires expertise in testing the user interface on mobile devices using tools like Appium or Perfecto and testing the API layer using tools like Postman, SOAP UI, or Rest Assured.

Quality engineers must be equipped with cloud-native testing capabilities for applications hosted on cloud platforms. This includes knowledge of Chaos testing, A/B testing, disaster recovery testing, performance testing, and other relevant techniques. This is a major transformation in the skills dimension of a Quality Engineer where they need to possess combination skills in testing across the web, mobile, microservices, cloud with a thorough understanding of Performance and Data testing.

Automate Everything, Everywhere by Everyone

The Growing Importance of Automation in Quality Engineering: In a world where efficiency is key, quality engineers must embrace automation as a core component of their practices. By automating repetitive activities and expanding their automation skills, these professionals can meet the ever-increasing demand for streamlined processes and deliver exceptional results in the fast-paced software industry.

Embracing Automation

Automation is the core of quality engineering practice to influence speed to production, efficiency and effectiveness of application delivery. Whether we apply Hyper Automation or incremental automation strategy, Quality engineers look for end to end automation using hybrid framework.

Extensive Automation

Clients expect Quality Engineers to automate every possible activity that is repeatable. They expect higher productivity gains from them to accommodate more deliverables.

Quality engineers play a vital role in Agile delivery, ensuring high-quality software at every phase. They possess overlapping skills with developers, allowing for collaboration and shared responsibilities. Multi-dimensional testing skills and adapting to changing technologies are becoming increasingly important. Lastly, automation has become a cornerstone of quality engineering practices, demanding that quality engineers possess the skills to automate processes effectively.

AI and Quality Engineering: Embracing the Power of Artificial Intelligence

In the previous sections, we discussed how the role of quality engineers is evolving with the changing landscape of technology. As Artificial Intelligence (AI) complements technology at a fast pace, it has influenced quality engineering methods and processes. Let us explore how AI can augment and automate quality engineering tasks, improving productivity and providing valuable insights. Additionally, we will discuss the importance of quality engineering when evaluating AI-based solutions and the parameters to consider in ensuring their quality. Quality engineering is a service offered to clients for assessing the quality of their products or processes. With the integration of AI, the client experience in quality engineering can be significantly enhanced. AI can empower quality engineers by providing insightful inputs that can boost their productivity.

These inputs may include the following:

- Advanced Analytics: AI can leverage sophisticated analytics techniques to analyze vast amounts of quality metrics, defects, and performance data. By extracting meaningful patterns and trends from this data, AI can offer valuable insights to quality engineers, enabling them to make data-driven decisions and improvements.

- Predictive Analytics: AI can employ predictive models to anticipate potential quality issues or defects in advance. By analyzing historical data, AI can identify patterns and factors that contribute to quality issues, helping quality engineers take proactive measures to prevent or mitigate such issues in the future.

- Automation and Efficiency: AI can automate repetitive and time-consuming tasks within the quality engineering process. By automating activities such as test case generation, test execution, and defect analysis, AI can free up quality engineers' time, allowing them to focus on more strategic and value-added activities.

- Real-time Monitoring: AI can provide real-time monitoring and alerts for quality-related metrics and indicators. This enables quality engineers to promptly identify deviations or anomalies, allowing them to take immediate action and ensure continuous quality improvement.

- Intelligent Recommendations: AI can analyze quality data and generate recommendations for process improvements or corrective actions. By identifying bottlenecks, inefficiencies, or areas of improvement, AI can assist quality engineers in making informed decisions to enhance the overall quality of the product or process.

As the technological landscape continues to evolve, Artificial Intelligence (AI) has emerged as a game-changer in quality engineering processes. In this section, we will discuss the impact of AI on quality engineering, exploring how it can augment and automate tasks, provide valuable insights, and improve productivity. Furthermore, we will delve into the crucial role of quality engineering in evaluating AI-based solutions, considering factors such as client expectations, prediction accuracy, explain ability, trustworthiness, and data security.

AI and Quality Engineering can be approached in two distinct contexts

As artificial intelligence continues to permeate various industries, its influence on quality engineering processes presents both opportunities and challenges. By understanding the dual context of AI in quality engineering and quality engineering for AI, professionals can harness the power of AI to augment, automate, and advise, while also addressing critical considerations for evaluating AI-based solutions, such as client expectations, prediction accuracy, explainability, trustworthiness, and data security.

AI in Quality Engineering

The integration of AI in Quality Engineering should enrich the client experience by providing valuable insights, speed of testing and automation. AI can empower quality engineers by offering inputs that enhance their productivity.
Some of the ways AI can achieve this are:

Augmentation

AI technology should enhance the role of a quality engineer by providing tools and capabilities to improve productivity. For instance, consider an AI-powered application that assists quality engineers in generating diverse test data. This data can be created synthetically based on structured and unstructured data from a training dataset. Quality engineers can ensure thorough testing by covering a wide range of scenarios by having access to such artificially generated data. This capability enhances their ability to identify potential issues and ensures the reliability and robustness of the tested software or system.

Automation

AI should automate manual tasks within quality engineering processes, making them more cost-effective and reducing time to market.
For example, imagine an AI-powered tool that allows quality engineers to

automatically convert Gherkin scripts (which provide structured input on application behavior) into Selenium code. The tool can analyze the Gherkin scripts and generate corresponding Selenium code by leveraging AI technology. This code can then be customized and used for automated test case execution, streamlining the testing process and saving valuable time and effort for the quality engineers.

Advisory

AI technology should provide insights and recommendations to quality engineers, empowering them to make informed decisions. Consider a scenario where an AI-based solution analyzes defect patterns in software development. Using this analysis, the AI system can provide valuable recommendations to the delivery team on proactive measures to prevent similar defects from occurring in future releases. By leveraging the insights provided by AI, the delivery team can take corrective actions, such as refining development processes, enhancing code quality, or addressing specific areas prone to defects. This proactive approach helps improve overall software quality and reduces the likelihood of recurring issues, leading to more reliable and efficient software releases. Extend the above scenario to include the predicted trends based on root cause of the defects. Taking historical patterns into consideration and predicting the defect trends for current projects will provide the quality engineers with the capability to plan their work better.

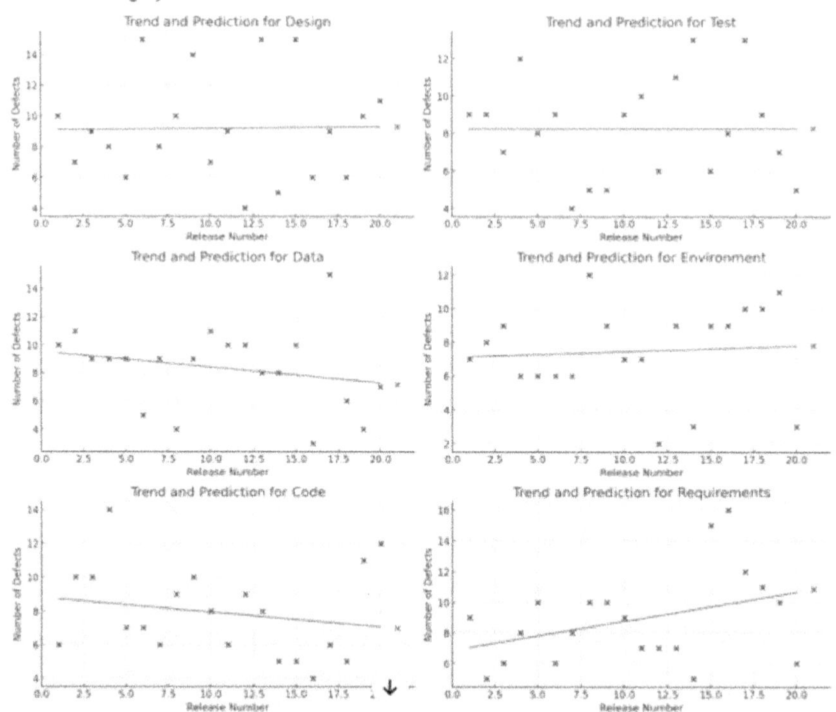

Figure 1.3: A sample predicted defect trends by defect root cause using AI

Quality Engineering for AI

As AI tech increasingly impacts our lives, evaluating the quality of AI-based solutions becomes crucial. Applying quality engineering processes becomes essential to validate and ensure the reliability of these solutions. Traditionally, quality engineering practices have been designed for deterministic systems. However, AI-based applications are probabilistic, requiring different capabilities to evaluate their quality.

Some critical considerations for quality engineering in the context of AI include:

Fulfilling Client Expectations

Applications utilizing AI technology should align with the client's requirements as specified. In the context of predicting the probability of a team's win in a cricket match, the application should perform as expected. For instance, the AI model should deliver reliable outcomes if the client expects accurate predictions based on various factors, such as team composition, past performance, and match conditions.

Accuracy of Predictions

The accuracy of the AI component's predictions should meet acceptable threshold levels. Using the example of cricket match prediction, the probability of the prediction should come with a confidence score more significant than a specified threshold, such as 90%, as defined in the specifications. To ensure the accuracy of the predictions, statistical validation can be performed by testing the model with multiple data points, including historical match data and relevant variables.

Explain-ability and Compliance

The outcome of the AI component should be explainable and consistent with the input data used for prediction. In the case of cricket match win predictability, the prediction outcome should align with the input features on which it was based. For example, if the AI model considers cloudy weather conditions as a factor that increases the probability of a win for the England team, the prediction should reflect this relationship. This ensures transparency and provides stakeholders with a clear understanding of how the prediction was made.

Trustworthiness and Avoidance of Unacceptable Information

AI-infused applications (AIIA) should be trustworthy and not provide any unacceptable or biased information. In the context of cricket match predictability, the outcome should not be influenced by non-related inputs or biases, such as endorsements from players advocating for the win of a particular team. The AI model should adhere to fair and unbiased algorithms to maintain the integrity of the predictions.

Data Security

The data security used to train the AI model should comply with the client's security policies. In the cricket match win prediction example, the features influencing the prediction, such as team statistics and match conditions, should be handled and stored securely, following the client's data security guidelines. Access to this data should only be restricted to authorized personnel, preventing unauthorized sharing or exposure.

AI has revolutionized quality engineering processes, offering augmentation, automation, and advisory capabilities. Quality engineering is critical in evaluating the quality of AI-infused applications, considering factors such as client expectations, accuracy of predictions, explainability, trustworthiness, and data security. By embracing the power of AI and applying quality engineering practices, organizations can ensure the delivery of high-quality and reliable AI-based solutions

Conclusion

In the world of Quality Engineering in the era of AI, we have explored the evolution of quality engineering and recognized its crucial role in the current technology landscape. Quality engineers have expanded their roles beyond traditional testing and are now actively involved in ensuring quality throughout the entire product lifecycle. This shift underscores the importance of continuous quality evaluation and its influence on the success of a product. Quality Engineering is no longer confined to the final stages of development or executed solely as part of gating phases; it has become an integral part of every phase, from requirements gathering to design, development, and deployment an integral part of every phase, from requirements gathering to design, development, and deployment. Furthermore, we have gained an overview of the impact of AI on quality engineering. AI has brought significant advancements and possibilities, enhanced the client experience and improved the productivity of quality engineers. By leveraging insights, automation, and advisory services through AI, quality engineers can deliver higher-quality outcomes more efficiently. This chapter emphasized associating AI and Quality Engineering in two different contexts. Firstly, AI in Quality Engineering focuses on leveraging AI technologies to enhance the quality engineering process, enabling quality engineers to improve their productivity and efficiency. Secondly, Quality Engineering for AI highlights the necessity of applying quality engineering practices specifically to AI-based solutions, considering their probabilistic nature and unique evaluation requirements. In summary, Quality Engineering involves ensuring that quality is built into every phase of the product lifecycle, from requirements gathering to design, development, and deployment. It is not limited to the final stages but is integral to every step, ensuring products meet high standards throughout. AI brings significant advancements to Quality Engineering by enhancing productivity and efficiency through automation and insights. Leveraging AI technologies allows quality engineers to improve their processes, and applying quality engineering practices to AI-based solutions ensures these complex systems are reliable and effective. As we move forward, the synergy between AI and Quality Engineering will continue to shape the future of technology, driving innovation and excellence in product development.

Exercise: Test Your Understanding

Answer the following questions and test your understanding of learning from `Chapter 1`:

Q. 1. What is one of the roles of Quality Engineers in Agile delivery?

    A. Writing code during development

    B. Evaluating sprint deliverables and developing automated test scripts

    C. Managing project timelines and resources

    D. Designing user interfaces

Q. 2. How can AI be applied to enhance the productivity of quality engineers in terms of test data generation?

    A. By developing traditional test scripts

    B. By manually creating diverse test data sets

    C. By automating the conversion of Gherkin scripts into Selenium code

    D. By conducting manual analysis of defect patterns

Q. 3. Why is it important for AI-infused applications to be trustworthy?

    A. To increase development speed

    B. To adhere to client security policies

    C. To provide biased information

    D. To ensure transparency in predictions

Q. 4. What is a crucial consideration for quality engineering in the context of AI-based solutions?

    A. Project timelines and milestones

    B. Predicting team wins in sports

    C. Avoiding client expectations

    D. Explainability and consistency in AI predictions

Q. 5. In the context of quality engineering for AI, what does "explainability" refer to?

    A. Explaining team wins in sports

    B. Providing biased information

    C. Explaining the outcome of AI predictions

    D. Developing Gherkin scripts

Chapter 2

Fundamentals of AI for Quality Engineers

The term Artificial intelligence (AI) triggers thoughts around data and analysis of the data to infer meaningful outcomes. Artificial intelligence tries to mimic the human mind and its cognitive functions like learning, problem-solving, and so on to predict certain behaviors. The essential function of AI here is to be able to get help in executing specific tasks that a human would usually do. This function helps us save time and utilize data to deliver tasks predictably based on large volumes of data. In this book, we will try to unravel another aspect of AI – validating expected behavior through Quality engineering! We will move from a 'predictive' aspect of AI to an 'expected' aspect of AI.In the previous chapter, the fundamentals of Quality Engineering (QE) was discussed in detail. This chapter will introduce you to basics of Artificial Intelligence (AI) and where it can be applied. It will also delve into application of AI in quality engineering process optimization. Understanding the pros and cons of incorporating AI in QE processes and how to address them. Let us familiarize ourselves with some terminologies and concepts of AI.

In this chapter, we will discuss the following topics:

- Understanding the basics of AI and its various applications
- Evolution of AI in Quality Engineering
- Role of AI in Optimizing and Automating Quality Engineering Processes
- Pros and Cons of Incorporating AI in Quality Engineering Practices
- Familiarizing Quality Engineers with AI Terminology and Concepts

Understanding the basics of AI and its various applications

In this section, we will understand the basics of Artificial Intelligence (AI). These will serve as the foundation for further understanding of the concepts presented in the later chapters.

Defining AI and its Core Principles

Artificial Intelligence refers to training machines to demonstrate human-like intelligence. This is done by simulating human intelligence and programming machines to perform tasks that a human can. Some common examples of the intelligence applied by AI are speech recognition, language translation, automated decision-making based on gathered data or insights.

We can see AI applied in several aspects of our day to life. In the digital world, all the marketing offers, or content recommendations are the functions of application of AI. In agriculture, the amount of content (like fertilizer and water) to be applied is a function of AI and Internet of Things (IoT).

Although not very new, AI is still evolving in the IT industry, complimenting and enhancing technology and its applications. The immense capabilities of AI remain unexplored even today and new breakthroughs are happening even as we go through this book. However, the core principles that drive the capabilities of AI remain essentially the same as discussed here. There must be a good degree of fairness in AI systems. The outcomes produced by AI systems must be fair to all individuals and rise above discrimination. It should come up with a neutral and fair judgment, mitigating biases, in data. If any error leads to undesirable consequences, the system should be accountable and able to address it. There should be an evident and explainable approach to how the outcome has been arrived at. Hence, AI systems must be transparent. Data Privacy is of utmost importance. Personal and Sensitive Personal Information (SPI) should be handled responsibly so that an individual's privacy is not compromised. It should also ensure that there is no unauthorized access to sensitive data that results in misuse. AI systems should also be robust to avoid any attacks by hackers, thereby compromising security. The system should be resilient to such attacks and continue performing even in adverse conditions. In short, it is of prime importance that the system be fail-safe! On the other hand, the AI system itself should also not cause any harm to the users. AI systems should comply with regulatory norms and laws and function within the legal framework. While AI systems are built to demonstrate human-like intelligence, they should augment the capabilities of humans and enhance their experience. Finally,

AI systems should aim to impact society positively. These core principles set a high benchmark for any AI system or application. An equally robust quality check is needed to ensure that the benchmark is met. Therefore, the role of Quality Engineers becomes very significant in ensuring that AI applications are inspected, validated, and verified, keeping the core principles of AI in mind. Educating quality engineers on testing AI applications is imperative, as the expected result for the AI system is much more than meets the eye.

Let's understand all the above, aspects in the context of implementing an AI solution in an e-commerce application:

- The AI-driven recommendation engine should suggest products based on user preferences and behaviors rather than biased data that could lead to unfair suggestions. If errors occur, the system should be accountable and capable of addressing any adverse consequences.

- If an AI system recommends certain products to a user, it should be able to explain the factors and data points that influenced its suggestions, such as past purchases, search history, and user ratings. This transparency helps build trust and allows users to understand and verify AI's decision-making processes.

- AI application must ensure that customer data, including purchase history and payment information, is securely stored and accessed only by authorized personnel, preventing any unauthorized use or data breaches.

- The AI-powered fraud detection system should detect and counteract fraudulent activities without compromising its performance. Similarly, the AI system itself should not cause harm to users, ensuring safe and reliable operation.

- The AI system must adhere to data protection regulations such as GDPR, ensuring ethical and legal handling of customer data.

- AI-powered chatbots can assist customers with their inquiries and guide them through the purchasing process, allowing customer service representatives to focus on more complex issues.

- AI applications can optimize supply chain logistics, reducing waste and improving efficiency, which can lead to lower prices for consumers and a smaller environmental footprint.

Narrow AI vs General AI vs Generative AI

There are two main types of Artificial Intelligence – Narrow AI (or Weak AI) and General AI (or Strong AI).

Narrow AI

As the name indicates, Narrow AI has a specific or narrow purpose. It is designed and programmed to perform a particular task. A 'defect' prediction system uses machine learning algorithms to analyze historical data from software development projects. By examining patterns and correlations in the data, the system can predict the likelihood of defects in new code. This helps quality engineers focus their testing efforts on the most vulnerable areas, improving efficiency and effectiveness. This system is considered Narrow AI because it is specifically designed to predict software defects. It excels in this task but lacks the ability to perform unrelated activities, such as writing a memo or engaging in general problem-solving. Its intelligence is confined to defect prediction and doesn't extend beyond that domain.

General AI

On the other hand, general AI, as the name indicates, is designed to perform several general tasks or a wide range of functions. It can understand, learn, and perform several tasks like humans using intelligence to do these tasks. Consider an AI system capable of writing an official memo. This AI can understand the context and purpose of the memo, gather relevant information, structure the content logically, and use appropriate language and tone. It can handle various aspects of writing, such as grammar, style, and coherence, and can adapt to different types of memos, whether they are formal, informal, or technical. This system is categorized as General AI because it demonstrates a broader understanding and versatility. It can perform multiple complex tasks that require cognitive abilities like human intelligence. Writing an official memo involves comprehension, creativity, and adaptability, all of which are hallmarks of General AI. comprehension, creativity, and adaptability. Unlike Narrow AI, which is limited to specific functions, General AI can apply its intelligence across diverse scenarios and tasks.

General AI

Generative AI is a third category of Artificial Intelligence that has emerged and become popular. As the name indicates, Generative AI can generate new content based on the context and knowledge it has been trained with, to perform several tasks. Currently, ChatGPT, Co-Pilot's, IBM's WatsonX are all the examples of Generative AI.

AI Techniques and Algorithms

Artificial Intelligence uses various techniques and algorithms to drive outcomes **(Fig 2.1)**.

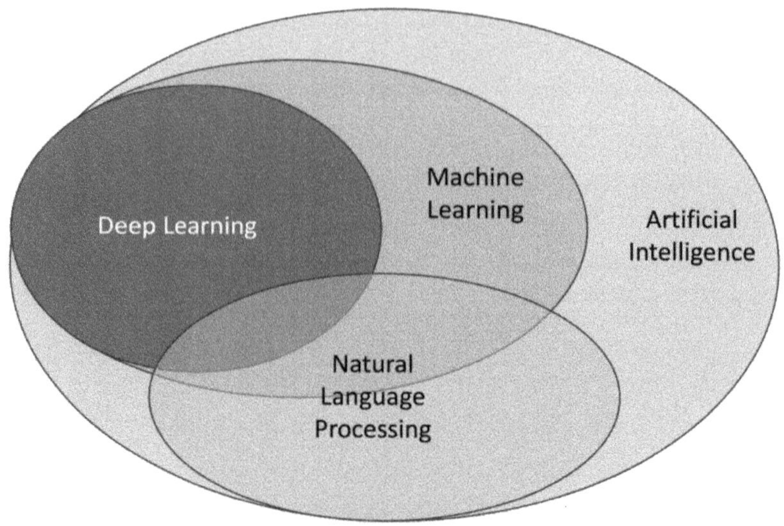

Figure 2.1: *Artificial Intelligence, Machine Learning, NLP and Deep Learning*

Some of the critical methods and algorithms are described below:

Machine Learning

Machine learning is a technique that uses data to build statistical models and algorithms. These models and algorithms help the computer or AI system learn from them and predict outcomes that help decision-making. As more data is fed into the system, the models identify patterns and relationships in the data, learn from them, and use this pattern recognition to predict outcomes and make decisions on new and unseen data. The IT programmer does not need to explicitly write programs and keep building logic with new data to arrive at the expected outcomes. Let us see a simple example to understand this better. If you have used any email application, you may have observed that certain emails are automatically pushed to the spam folder. The email user may often create rules to move some emails into the spam folder, e.g., move all emails received from a particular online retail shopping site to the spam folder. However, it is tough for the user to keep on adding rules for every spam email received from different domains. To resolve the situation, the email app uses machine learning to identify keywords and phrases that help understand if an email is spam and automatically moves it to the spam folder. This reduces the manual effort that the user may have had to spend otherwise. In this case, the data set used by machine learning to learn from are spam emails from various sources. The model understands the pattern of spam emails and uses keywords to identify and differentiate between spam and useful emails.

In the real world, machine learning models can be much more complex and use large data sets with complex patterns and relationships to learn:

- **Supervised Learning**: In this type of Learning, the machine learning model uses a structured and labeled data set with well-defined input and the corresponding output. This involves mapping the input with the corresponding output. With this mapping done, the model can predict outcomes based on the underlying mapping. The identification and filtering of spam emails is an example of Supervised Learning

- **Unsupervised Learning**: This type of Learning involves unlabeled data where the algorithm tries to identify patterns and relationships within the data. It helps predict outcomes and decision-making based on these patterns. An example of unsupervised Learning is the study of customer behavior and preferences to understand and categorize customers for the targeted sales of commodities. You may have experienced marketing material being delivered to your mailbox or ads on your browser. The selection of ads and marketing material depends on your behavior and preferences as a customer. The AI system recognizes patterns in your activity on the internet and uses this unlabeled data to predict your areas of interest.

- **Reinforced Learning**: This is a type of Learning where an agent interacts with the environment and learns to make decisions. The agent acts and receives feedback in the form of rewards or penalties. The right decisions are those that maximize rewards. Several games make use of Reinforcement Learning, for example, online chess. It enhances the playing experience by making use of Reinforcement Learning to adjust the difficulty level of the game. The algorithm can also dynamically analyze the strategy of the opponent player and adapt its own strategy according to that in real time. This makes the playing experience even more interesting and challenging.

Deep Learning

Deep Learning focuses on artificial Neural Networks to solve complex problems. A Neural network is a concept in AI whose functioning behaves much like the human brain. It consists of layers of interconnected neurons or nodes. Each node is a feature of the input data. 'Deep' here indicates that there may be multiple hidden layers between the input and the output layer. The hidden layers perform computations on the input received and pass on the result to the next layer. The nodes in the output layer produce the outcome of the network. Deep Learning teaches a computer or an IT system to think and make its own decisions by training deep neural networks. Some examples where deep Learning is used are image and speech recognition, natural language processing, games.

Natural Processing Language

Natural Language Processing (NLP) is an AI concept that focuses on the interaction between a computer and a human. It helps the computer to understand the language spoken by the human, analyze and interpret it and generate a meaningful response. The most common examples of natural language processing are virtual assistants like Siri and Alexa. NLP as a technology is getting advanced continuously to make human-computer interaction more and more meaningful. AI is gradually bringing to life some of the magical concepts in many sci-fi movies of yesteryears. Artificial Intelligence, Machine Learning and Deep Learning are interrelated concepts. The figure below helps in understanding how they are related.

Commonly used algorithms in quality Engineering

Quality Engineering uses Algorithms and Artificial Intelligence for optimizing processes, improving efficiency and ensuring high-quality outcomes. The algorithm, as you know, is a step-by-step approach to solving a problem to achieve an outcome. Quality Engineering aims at ensuring the quality of the outcome by analyzing data, detecting patterns to predict failures, and validating and verifying the result.
Understanding commonly used algorithms in quality engineering helps organizations maintain efficiency and ensure high-quality outcomes. Below is an overview of these essential techniques:

Statistical Process Control (SPC) Algorithms

These algorithms monitor and control processes to maintain consistent quality.

- **Control Chart Algorithms**: Plot data points and set control limits to track process stability.

- **Run Chart Algorithms**: Visualize trends over time to identify patterns or anomalies.

Machine Learning Algorithms

Machine learning algorithms predict outcomes and uncover patterns in data.

- **Regression Algorithms**: Predict continuous variables using one or more input variables.

- **Classification Algorithms**: Categorize data into predefined groups, such as decision trees.
- **Clustering Algorithms**: Group similar data points for insights.
- **Anomaly Detection Algorithms**: Identify abnormal patterns or outliers in datasets.
- **Neural Networks Algorithms**: Solve complex problems like image or speech recognition.

Natural Language Processing (NLP) Algorithms

NLP techniques make sense of textual data to derive meaningful insights.

- Tokenization: Break down text into individual words or phrases (tokens).
- Named Entity Recognition (NER): Identify entity names, locations, and dates in text.
- Sentiment Analysis: Analyze the emotional tone expressed in the text.

Optimization Algorithms

These algorithms optimize outcomes by improving performance and minimizing errors.

- **Genetic Algorithms**: Use natural selection principles to find optimal solutions.
- **Simulated Annealing**: Find approximate global optima using probability-based optimization.
- **Gradient Descent**: Minimize machine learning error by iteratively adjusting model parameters.

Image and Signal Processing Algorithms

These techniques analyze and enhance visual and audio data.

- **Edge Detection**: Identify object boundaries in images.
- **Noise Reduction**: Eliminate unwanted distortions in signals or images.
- **Image Recognition**: Detect and classify objects within images.

Time Series Analysis Algorithms

Analyze data points collected over time to identify trends and make predictions.

- **ARIMA (AutoRegressive Integrated Moving Average)**: Model and forecast time series data.
- **Exponential Smoothing**: Predict future values by giving recent observations more weight.

Quality Control Algorithms

These methods focus on identifying root causes and improving processes.

- **Pareto Analysis**: Identify the most significant factors causing the majority of problems.
- **Ishikawa (Fishbone) Diagrams**: Visualize potential causes to identify the root issue.

Monte Carlo Simulation

A powerful tool that uses random sampling to predict probabilities of different outcomes.

These algorithms are essential at various stages of quality engineering to analyze data, detect patterns, and predict potential failures—ensuring consistent, high-quality results.

Quality Engineers need to understand AI from two aspects:

- Leveraging AI in QE to analyze large datasets, identify trends, potential defects, and improvement areas, and automate test processes. That is, use the power of AI to test applications, processes, and systems (Described above).
- Leveraging QE to check the quality of AI applications/models. That is, testing the AI applications and systems (discussed later in this chapter).

Evolution of AI in Quality Engineering

Businesses are rapidly adopting AI-based solutions in all spheres of life. Competition in the market has grown many-fold, and clients are now turning to AI to gain that extra edge to compete for the top spot. AI-based solutions are redefining digitization. Today, end users are much more demanding and creative in laying down their problem statements. This has led to businesses turning to Artificial Intelligence to solve the unsolvable problems. Given the benefits of AI solutions, CXOs are willing to invest in them. A wide variety of business problems that were unexplored thus far have come to the fore, leading to a rise in opportunities. A variety of Open-Source, off-the-shelf, and packaged solutions are becoming available in the market, leading to a rise in competition. However, there are several challenges in adopting AI solutions as well. The biggest challenge is the inability to explain the predictions or outcomes produced by Deep learning models, which appear to be black boxes today. Secondly, there are concerns about biases introduced due to the unavailability of adequate and diverse datasets for training the models. The availability of good-quality data and a significant volume of data has always been a challenge, especially for AI systems that rely heavily on data sets for training the models. Today, there is also a need for a well-defined testing process for AI-based solutions. Hence, testing is often limited to unit testing. These market trends are heavily driving Artificial Intelligence Application Testing, and the later chapters of this book will focus more closely on this.

Role of AI in Optimizing and Automating Quality Engineering Processes

AI plays a significant role in optimizing and automating quality engineering processes and the entire software development lifecycle.

Let's look at some aspects of Quality Engineering where AI plays a pivotal role:

Test Automation

Test Automation is the process of automating the design and execution of test cases that would otherwise be run manually, with a user invoking each step of the test case and comparing the actual result against the expected result. AI helps in the creation and execution of automated test scripts. The automated and smarter way of test execution increases efficiency and provides better coverage. Test script generation using AI techniques can reduce the effort by 15-20% with 70-80% accuracy over a period.

The benefits of test automation are manifold:

- Faster test design and execution.
- Reduced manual error.
- Better test coverage.
- Early feedback on the quality of the work product.

Test Case Generation

Test Case Generation is the process of documenting test cases, which consist of steps for execution along with the expected result at each step. AI algorithms can be used to intelligently and automatically generate test cases based on the code and requirements and optimize them.

The benefits of intelligent test case generation are:

- Faster creation of test cases.
- Adequate test coverage.
- Early identification of potential issues in the application.

Defect Prediction and Prevention

Defect prediction predicts the number of defects expected to be encountered during testing. Defect prediction helps estimate the time to complete the test cycle and improve the code quality based on the feedback. Defect prevention is taking action to ensure minimal defects are encountered during testing by eliminating them early in the cycle. 30-40% of the defects can be prevented using AI. AI can help to predict the areas in the application that are vulnerable and prone to defects and suggest preventive steps to avoid these defects. It accomplishes this by analyzing historical data.

The benefits of AI-driven Defect Prediction and Prevention are:

- Early redressal of potential quality issues in the application.
- Minimize the number of defects introduced into the work product during development.

Performance Testing Optimization

Performance testing is a type of software testing that validates overall performance - response time, throughput, concurrency, network latency, etc.- under different scenarios. AI-driven performance testing determines the software's behavior under varying conditions, thereby optimizing the scenarios of performance testing.

The benefits of AI-driven Performance testing are:

- Ensure the application meets performance requirements in different scenarios.
- Helps to enhance performance by identifying issues, if any.

Dynamic Test Data Management

To perform testing, we must have test data to match every possible scenario. This helps ensure thorough testing under all scenarios, thereby providing better coverage. Creating such test data is time-consuming, and some scenarios will be left behind due to oversight. AI helps generate and manage the test data for the application as per the requirements. Generating synthetic data using AI can reduce the test data provisioning effort by 20-30%.

The benefits of AI-driven Test data management are:

- Saves time needed for creating test data manually.
- Helps to provide better test coverage by ensuring data is available for all scenarios as per requirement.
- AI-generated test data ensures robust testing.

Automated Regression Testing

Regression Testing ensures that changes made do not adversely impact the overall application. Some of the existing test cases are selected and re-executed to validate this. AI-driven regression testing ensures the selection of the relevant test cases to validate the impact of code changes. Using AI techniques, the test design effort to generate a regression test suite can be reduced by 70%.
The benefits of AI-driven Automated Regression testing are:

- Expedite validation of application stability.
- Relevant test case selection for regression.

Root Cause Analysis

To resolve an issue fully, it is essential to identify the root cause. Manually stepping through the 5-Why process or a fishbone diagram can be used to identify the root cause. However, AI-driven analysis of the issue and the test results can significantly expedite the root cause identification process. Based on industry experience, using AI can reduce root-cause analysis efforts by approximately 40%.
The benefits of AI-driven Root Cause Analysis are:

- Expedite troubleshooting of issues
- Reduced MTTR (Mean time to resolve)
- Ensure stable application

Natural Language Processing (NLP) for Test Documentation

Test documentation is an integral part of the test process. Often, it is a manual effort that requires time to create and maintain. Natural Language Processing (NLP) can help create and analyze test documentation, reducing documentation efforts by up to 30%.
Having relevant test documentation has several benefits:

- Streamlined test documentation process

- Well-defined requirements
- Better communication with stakeholders

Automated Test Environment Setup

Before application testing can commence, a test environment needs to be set up. Ideally, it should be production-like and separate from the development environment to ensure a clean environment to start testing. AI can help automate the setup and provisioning of the test environment, which would otherwise have been a manual process. With an automated approach, it is possible to spin up the test environment as often as needed. AI-driven environment setup can reduce efforts by approximately 15-25%.

Automated Test Environment setup helps with:

- Time saved in setup and provisioning of environment
- More consistent and standardized approach for setup
- Reduced errors and inconsistencies

Continuous Monitoring and Feedback

Continuous monitoring and feedback are the essence of continuous improvement. AI-enabled automated monitoring and feedback help get real-time insights and feedback on the application. These insights can be applied to make the application more robust. AI can enhance monitoring and feedback efficiency by up to 40%.

The benefits of AI-enabled automated monitoring and feedback are:

- Continuous improvement
- Early identification of issues
- Faster release cycles

Pros and Cons of Incorporating AI in Quality Engineering Practices

AI offers many advantages in Quality Engineering. At a high level, it improves the overall efficiency of the test process. The velocity of testing increases many-fold with AI enabled automated test execution. It also helps to provide better test coverage and better reliability by being able to identify defects accurately.

Advantages of AI in Quality Engineering process

Below is a listing of the various advantages of incorporating AI in Quality Engineering processes.

- Efficiency in test automation
- Efficient defect prevention by leveraging predictive analytics
- Intelligent and smarter test case generation providing optimum coverage
- Better Test data management
- Enhanced and easy to do Performance Testing
- Intelligent selection of relevant regression suite
- Smarter Regression test execution
- Automated provisioning, configuration and setup of test environment
- Continuous monitoring and feedback
- Efficient and effective utilization of resources
- AI assisted and enhanced Security Testing
- Dynamic test strategies
- Faster time-to-market
- Better decision making

Challenges and Risks

As we have seen, there are several advantages of incorporating AI in Quality Engineering. However, there are a few risks and challenges also that one must be aware of. This helps in making an informed decision. The biggest challenge is the inability to explain the predictions, or the outcomes produced by Deep Learning models, which function as a black box today. This can however be mitigated by using simpler models in case there is a business need for transparency. Secondly, there are concerns around biases introduced due to unavailability of adequate and diverse datasets for training the models. AI models can end up learning biases and discrimination if they are present in the training data. As a result, the outcome produced by such models can be discriminatory or reflect biasness. Bias detection tools can be used to mitigate this issue. Also, continuous monitoring of data for fairness during training is a recommended approach for mitigation. The availability of good quality data and significant volume of data has always been a challenge, especially for AI systems that rely heavily on data sets for training the models. If AI models are not secure, they may pose a threat to security and privacy. Hence, it is important to anonymize and encrypt data. It is also necessary to incorporate ethical guidelines to avoid unintentional adverse impact of decision making. Adherence to regulatory requirements, which may change over time, also requires continuous compliance measures to be implemented to avoid any issues. Relying on the automated approach without due diligence may sometimes result in issues due to oversight or negligence. Hence, it is sometimes critical to combine automated testing with manual testing to balance AI with human expertise, especially when testing a critical and unique scenario for the first time. Another challenge that organizations face is the scarcity of skilled quality engineers who possess both AI and testing skills. Hence, organizations invest in training their staff and ensuring that talent is transformed and remains current in the industry. When applications undergo changes, and AI models are not re-trained, they may end up becoming obsolete and their performance may deteriorate. This phenomenon is referred to as model decay. To avoid this, it is important to continuously update and re-train the models and implement continuous Learning. Today, there is also a lack of a well-defined testing process for AI-based solutions. Hence, testing is often limited to unit testing.

Leveraging Quality Engineering to check quality of AI applications/models

To overcome the challenges and risks, it is crucial to test and validate the AI models for accuracy, fairness, robustness and performance. However, testing of AI models has never been straightforward. Let us try to understand how AI models can be tested for quality. The first step towards testing any software or work product is to understand the architecture of the software, followed by the development lifecycle. Figure 2.2 shows a typical architecture of AI-enabled applications. Understanding this architecture is integral to testing it.

AI application architecture consists of the following key components:

- **Data Ingestion engine**: The data ingestion engine is responsible for collecting, consolidating and processing raw data from various sources to train the AI model. This data is related to the domain in which one is trying to train the model. The data ingestion engine transfers the data to a database.

- **Database layer**: The database component stores the processed and unprocessed data ingested by the AI system.

- **Data Pre-processing engine**: Data ingested by the AI system in raw form must be pre-processed, i.e. cleaned and normalized, before it can be used by the AI model. This component is responsible for pre-processing raw data.

- **Machine Learning Models** are at the heart of AI systems. AI models are trained with the help of labelled data sets which teach it to learn and recognize patterns and make predictions that can help in decision making. The training infrastructure may comprise of powerful computing resources like GPUs (Graphics Processing Unit).

If models are at the heart of the AI systems, Inference Engine breathes life into the AI system! With the help of the trained model, it identifies patterns and relationships in the data, learns from them and uses this pattern recognition to predict outcomes and make decisions on new and unseen data. To use the AI system, APIs are exposed to integrate and communicate between different components and external systems.

A User Interface provides a user-friendly mechanism for users to interact with the AI application. A Feedback Loop is a key component that helps in continuous Learning of the AI model. A mechanism of collecting feedback from real-world users provides a means of re-training the model.

In addition to these key components, the architecture also has features for monitoring and logging, Security and Privacy, scalability, governance and other non-functional requirements (**Fig.2.2**).

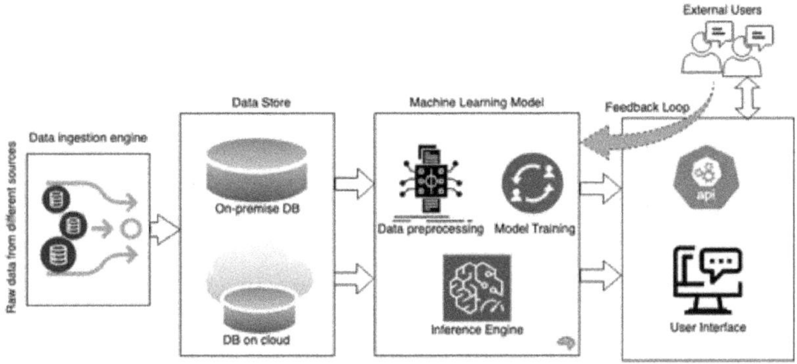

Figure 2.2: *Architecture of AI Application*

The architecture of an AI application has 3 key components that offer opportunity for validation:

- **Data**: the training data is a key ingredient for training the AI Model. Hence, it is necessary to analyze and test the accuracy of the training data. This helps to validate the predictability of the training data.

- **Machine Learning Model:** The machine learning model needs to be tested for two things – accuracy of the outcome produced, and integration with other components of the application to deliver the outcome

- **User Interface**: The user interface is the interface where the model outcome can be presented to the end user. Hence, it is necessary to test the visual representation.

Development lifecycle of Machine Learning Models

Now that we have understood the high-level architecture of an AI application, let us see what the development lifecycle of these models looks like (**Fig 2.3**).

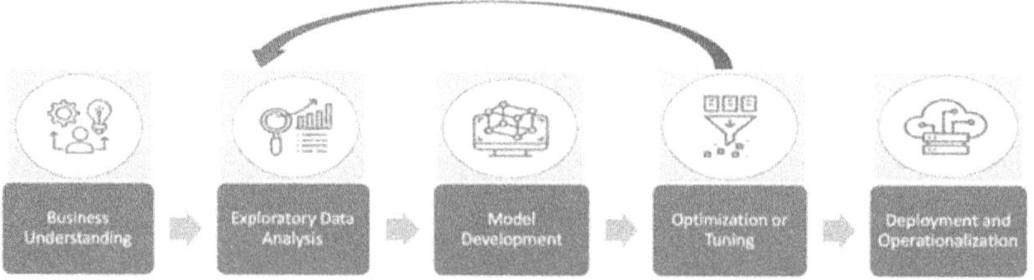

Figure 2.3: Architecture of AI Application

Th development lifecycle comprises of the following stages and activities:

- Business Understanding
    - o Understanding business objectives
    - o Requirements analysis
- Exploratory Data Analysis
    - o Understanding the business inputs/data through data visualization
    - o Understanding the relationship between input data and expected output (Feature Engineering)
- Model Development

    - o Data pre-processing strategy and development
    - o Machine Learning algorithm selection
    - o Model development
    - o Statistical evaluation of the model.
    - o Integration with other components of the solution

- Optimization or Tuning
    - o Optimizing the model to suit the requirement.
    - o Performance optimization
    - o Delivering the integrated solution for testing.
- Deployment and Operationalization

    - o Deploy the solution in production environment.
    - o Operationalize the usage of the solution.

Once we have established the development lifecycle, we need to identify the workflow of testing activities and align them with the development lifecycle (**Fig 2.4**).

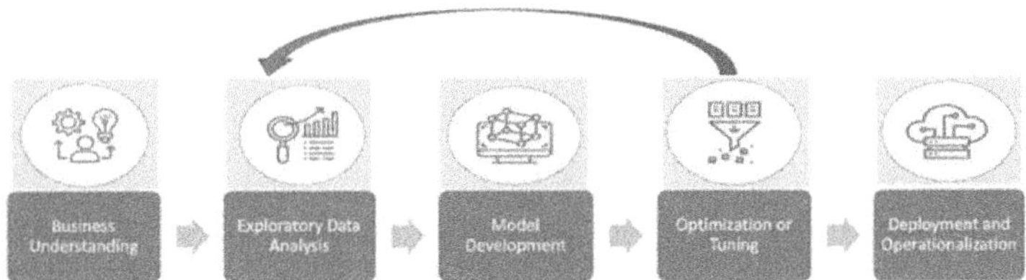

***Figure 2.4**: Test Lifecycle*

Below is a list of test activities in the testing lifecycle of Machine Learning models:

- Training Data Analysis: This is a critical step in the testing process, as the quality of training data impacts the performance of the model. Below are some of the considerations in this step:
    o Evaluate the Quality of Machine Learning Training Data
    o Validate data against regulatory compliances
    o Plug any missing data to prevent biases and discrimination
    o The dataset should be large enough to capture the complexity
    o Ensure that data is accurate and consistent
    o Monitor continuously to avoid model drift
    o Data must be relevant
- Test Data Analytics
    o Evaluate the Quality of Machine Learning Test Data after the machine learning model is ready for testing.
    o Generate synthetic test data, if data is found to be inadequate.
- Test Case Optimization
    o Use techniques like Combinatorial Test Design (CTD) to optimize test cases to provide complete coverage
- Test Data Generation
    o Generate data for test case scenarios
    o Fetch data specification from Optimized test cases to generate synthetic test data
- Test Execution Automation
    o Automate the test cases obtained from the Combinatorial Model.
    o Execute the automated test cases
- Test Result Validation
    o Validate the test results using statistical methods.

  o When the results are as per business expectations, sign off to deploy the solution.

Familiarizing Quality Engineers with AI Terminology and Concepts

In this section, we will define some basic terminologies and concepts for your preliminary understanding. These concepts will be used in later chapters as we learn more about AI in testing:

- **Artificial Intelligence**: The term Artificial Intelligence refers to training machines to demonstrate human-like intelligence.

- **Narrow AI:** As the name indicates, Narrow AI has a very specific or narrow purpose. It is designed and programmed to perform a very specific task.

- **General AI**: General AI, as the name indicates, is designed to be able to perform several general tasks, or a wide range of functions. It can understand, learn and perform several tasks like humans using intelligence to do these tasks.

- **Generative AI**: As the name indicates, Generative AI can generate new content based on the context and knowledge that it has been trained with to perform several tasks.

- **Machine Learning (ML)** is a technique that uses data to build statistical models and algorithms. These models and algorithms help the computer or AI system to learn from them and predict outcomes that help in decision-making. Machine Learning is a subset of Artificial Intelligence which involves the creation of algorithms and models that can learn patterns and use that to make predictions or support decision making.

- **Supervised Learning**: In this type of Learning, the machine learning model uses and structured and labelled data set with well-defined input and corresponding output. This involves mapping the input with the corresponding output. With this mapping done, the model can predict outcomes based on the underlying mapping.

- **Unsupervised Learning:** This type of Learning involves unlabeled data where the algorithm tries to identify patterns and relationships within the data. It helps in predicting outcomes and decision making based on these patterns.

- **Reinforced Learning**: This is a type of Learning where an agent interacts with the environment and learns to make decisions. The agent takes action and receives feedback in the form of rewards or penalties. The right decisions are those that maximize rewards.

- **Deep Learning** focuses on artificial Neural Networks to solve complex problems. A Neural network is a concept in AI whose functioning behaves much like the human brain. It consists of layers of interconnected neurons or nodes. Each node is a feature of the input data. 'Deep' here indicates that there may be multiple hidden layers between the input and the output layer. The hidden layers perform computations on the input received and pass on result to the next layer. The nodes in the output layer produce the outcome of the network.

- **Natural Language processing** is an AI concept that focuses on interaction between a computer and human. It helps the computer to understand the language spoken by the human, analyze and interpret it and generate a meaningful response.

- **Tokenization** refers to the process of breaking down text into smaller units or tokens, e.g. individual words or phrases.

- **Over-representation** is a type of bias in data where certain classes or categories are not represented sufficiently enough in the dataset as compared to the real world. Models trained with such data demonstrate biasness and hence better performance in majority classes. However, the model performs poorly on minority classes that have not been represented proportionately.

- **Under-representation** is a type of bias in data where certain classes or categories are represented less than they should be when compared to their occurrence in the real world. Models trained on under-represented dataset may not be able to make accurate predictions since they have not been able to learn how to recognize patterns properly for minority classes.

- **Feature Engineering**: The process of using raw data to select, transform, or create relevant features to enhance the performance of machine learning models is called Feature Engineering.

- **Overfitting:** When a machine learning model performs well when used with training data but not as good with unseen data, it is said to be overfitting.

- **Underfitting**: When a model is too simple to identify patterns and hence performs poorly both on training as well as unseen data, it is said to be underfitting.

- **Model evaluation metrics:** Metrics such as accuracy, precision etc. used to measure the performance of a machine learning model are called Models evaluation metrics.

- **Named Entity Recognition (NER)**: It refers to the process of identifying entities such as names, places, dates etc. in text.

- **Sentiment Analysis:** This is the process of analyzing the sentiment expressed in textual data.

- **Explainable AI** systems designed in such a way that their outcomes and predictions can be understood and explained by humans are called Explainable AI or XAI.

- **True Positive**: When a model predicts a positive outcome, and the result is positive, then it is said to be true positive.

- **True Negative**: When a model predicts a negative outcome, and the result is negative, then it is said to be true negative.

- **False Positive**: When a model predicts a positive outcome, and the result is negative, then it is said to be false positive.

- **False Negative**: When a model predicts a negative outcome, and the result is positive, then it is said to be false positive.

- **Classification Model**: A type of machine learning model that is used to classify input data into different categories is called a classification model.

- **Confusion Matrix**: Confusion matrix is a table showing the number of true positives, true negatives, false positives, and false negatives. This is used to evaluate the performance of a classification model.

- **Labelled dataset**: A labelled data set is a collection of datapoints where each data point has both input features and corresponding output correct output.

Conclusion

In this chapter, we have learned the basic concept of Artificial intelligence and the various types of learning that a machine-learning model can undergo. We have understood the basic concepts of Artificial intelligence and how it applies to Quality Engineering in two ways – one in which AI is used to enhance the Quality engineering experience by applying AI to automate and accelerate the various stages and activities of Quality Engineering and two where Quality Engineering is applied to test AI applications themselves. We have also familiarized ourselves with some critical terminologies of Artificial Intelligence and how it plays a pivotal role in Quality Engineering today. This is a motivation for Quality Engineers to continuously enhance their skills to effectively do a quality check on age applications by applying new-age technology in Quality Engineering itself. We have also explored the fundamental principles of Artificial Intelligence and the different forms of learning that a machine learning model can undertake. We have grasped the essential ideas of Artificial Intelligence and its application to Quality Engineering in two aspects – one where AI is employed to improve the Quality Engineering experience by utilizing AI to automate and speed up the various stages and tasks of Quality Engineering, and another where Quality Engineering is used to examine AI applications.

Additionally, we have acquainted ourselves with some crucial terminology of Artificial Intelligence and its significant impact on Quality Engineering today. This serves as an inspiration for Quality Engineers to consistently develop their abilities to efficiently perform quality assessments on modern applications by implementing cutting-edge technology within Quality Engineering itself.

Exercise: Test Your Understanding

Answer the following questions and test your understanding of learning from Chapter 2:

Q. 1. Mention the different types of Learning that a machine learning model undergoes:

- A. Supervised Learning, Unsupervised Learning and Reinforced Learning
- B. Thorough Learning, Unsupervised Learning and Supervised Learning
- C. Reinforced Learning, Disciplined Learning, In-disciplined Learning
- D. Supervised learning, monitored learning, Reinforced Learning

Q. 2. AI applications can only be unit tested by Quality Engineers. True or false?

- A. True
- B. False

Q. 3. What is the difference between true positive and false positive?

- A. When a model predicts a positive outcome, and the result is negative, then it is said to be true positive. When a model predicts positive outcome, and the result is negative, then it is said to be false positive
- B. When a model predicts a positive outcome, and the result is positive, then it is said to be true positive. When a model predicts negative outcome, and the result is negative, then it is said to be false positive
- C. When a model predicts a positive outcome, and the result is positive, then it is said to be true positive. When a model predicts positive outcome, and the result is negative, then it is said to be false positive
- D. When a model predicts a negative outcome, and the result is positive, then it is said to be true positive. When a model predicts positive outcome, and the result is negative, then it is said to be false positive

Q. 4. What is data ingestion?

- A. Data ingestion is the process of collecting, consolidating, and processing raw data from various sources. This data is used to train the AI model
- B. Data ingestion is the process of saving data in the database

C. Data ingestion is the process of tokenizing data and persisting it in the data store

D. Data ingestion is the process of identification of various sources of data

Q. 5. What are some of the key considerations for training data analysis when developing a machine learning model?

A. Ensure that data is accurate, relevant and consistent

B. Ensure that it is easy to save data in the database

C. The dataset should be large enough to capture the complexity

D. Data should be only in text format

Chapter 3

Paradigm Shift: Evaluating Probabilistic AI Systems

Traditionally, Quality Engineering practices were targeted for testing and evaluating deterministic systems, which operate with a predictable and consistent output based on a given set of inputs. However, with the rapid adoption of Artificial Intelligence (AI) in various applications, there has been a notable shift towards systems that exhibit a more probabilistic nature. Probabilistic systems, unlike deterministic ones, produce outputs based on the likelihood of specific outcomes which introduces a new layer of complexity and uncertainty in their behavior.

As a result of this paradigm shift in applications being developed and tested, it has become increasingly necessary for Quality Engineering practices to be customized and adapted to suit these probabilistic AI systems. To effectively evaluate and ensure the quality of such applications, it is important to understand how they behave differently from deterministic systems. This chapter will delve into the unique characteristics of probabilistic AI systems, providing insights into their distinct behavior and offering guidance on tailoring Quality Engineering practices to assess their performance and reliability effectively.

In this chapter, we will discuss the following topics:

- Exploring the differences between deterministic and probabilistic AI Systems
- Challenges and considerations in evaluating the quality of probabilistic systems
- Statistical analysis techniques for evaluating probabilistic outputs

Exploring the differences between deterministic and probabilistic AI Systems

Deterministic and probabilistic applications are distinct systems that function based on different principles. To understand their differences, it is crucial to understand the definitions and characteristics of each type of application.

Deterministic applications

Deterministic applications, commonly found in traditional business systems, operate based on predefined outcomes determined by specific business rules or conditions. These rules and conditions are derived from inputs that influence the decisions made by the applications. The behavior and results of deterministic applications are predictable and consistent, as they follow a specific set of rules or guidelines to generate outcomes.

Let us understand this with an example of a payment gateway application in Financial Services.

Banks in India provide payment options by multiple modes at merchants site, i.e. credit cards, debit cards, internet banking and UPI gateway. The authentication process for each of these modes of payment, though different, is deterministic and pre-defined. These authentication rules are guided by regulatory organizations like Reserve Bank of India.

When a user selects a preferred payment method, the payment gateway application identifies the mode of payment and presents appropriate input fields for the user to provide the information. The payment gateway application defines a clear set of pre-defined authentication methods.

For example, Debit and Credit Card payments must be authenticated using card number, name on the card, expiry date and CVV code. In addition to these inputs, some payment gateways include the need for a one-time password (OTP) sent to the registered mobile number or email ID for additional authentication.

In the case of UPI payments, the process is slightly different. After selecting the UPI payment mode, users are asked to enter their UPI ID or select it from a linked account list. Once the UPI ID is provided, the application requests a Personal Identification Number (PIN) from the user. This PIN acts as a secure authentication code to authorize the transaction. When the user enters their PIN, the payment gateway application validates it and if correct, proceeds to process the transaction.

If you look at the process in the above example, the payment gateway application's behavior and responses are deterministic throughout these processes, governed by predefined business rules and conditions. The system consistently follows the established guidelines and procedures for each payment mode, resulting in predictable and consistent outcomes.

This is how deterministic applications function. It is important to understand their unique characteristics to evaluate their performance and reliability effectively. By acknowledging the deterministic nature of such systems, engineers and developers can better tailor quality engineering practices to suit these applications and ensure they meet the desired business objectives.

Deterministic applications possess the following characteristics:

- Outcomes are predefined based on specific business rules or conditions.

- Input directly influences the decisions made by the application.

- The behavior and results of the application are predictable and consistent.

- Deterministic systems are standard in traditional business applications, such as payment gateways.

Probabilistic Systems

The advent of artificial intelligence (AI) technology has introduced a significant shift in the decision-making process of IT systems, transitioning from deterministic to probabilistic behavior. Probabilistic applications, often associated with AI and machine learning (ML) systems, determine outcomes based on statistical probabilities, considering the most likely result given a set of inputs. These systems rely on complex mathematical and statistical computations, rendering their behavior less predictable than deterministic applications.

To function effectively, probabilistic systems require extensive training on a wide range of data and numerous data points to identify patterns within the information. The choice of algorithm used to predict outcomes depends on the specific business problem at hand. Unlike rule-based predictors, these systems employ intricate neural networks, regression algorithms and other advanced techniques.

One prominent example of a probabilistic application is the conversational AI systems, such as Alexa, Google Assistant and Siri. These virtual assistants are trained using vast amounts of data to determine the intent behind a user's query accurately. They are also equipped with an array of potential responses to various questions. These systems utilize machine learning algorithms like Natural Language Processing (NLP) to interpret the data and identify keywords.

Upon receiving a user's query, the AI system searches for the most likely question that matches the given keywords. If multiple questions are found with varying statistical confidence scores, the system selects the one with the highest score as the most probable response. If no suitable match is identified, the chatbot will request further information from the user to refine its search. This example highlights the probabilistic nature of AI and machine learning-infused applications, which differ significantly from deterministic systems.

Probabilistic applications exhibit the following characteristics:

- Outcomes are determined based on statistical probabilities rather than predefined rules.

- The behavior of these systems could be more predictable due to the use of complex mathematical and statistical computations.

- Probabilistic applications require extensive training on diverse data and many data points to identify patterns.

- The choice of algorithm depends on the specific business problem and can include advanced techniques like neural networks and regression algorithms.

- Examples of probabilistic systems include AI-based conversational assistants like Alexa, Google Assistant and Siri.

Understanding the distinctions between deterministic and probabilistic applications is essential for tailoring quality engineering practices to suit each type of system. By recognizing probabilistic systems' unique characteristics and behavior, engineers and developers can effectively assess their performance and reliability, ensuring that they meet the desired business objectives and provide users with accurate, contextually appropriate responses. Let us summarize the comparison between deterministic and probabilistic systems by identifying critical parameters. By understanding the differences between these two types of systems, engineers and developers can better tailor their quality engineering practices to evaluate their performance and reliability effectively.

Parameter	Deterministic Systems	Probabilistic Systems
Outcome determination	Based on predefined rules or conditions	Based on statistical probabilities
Predictability	Predictable and consistent	Less predictable due to complex computations
Data requirements	Not always data-driven	Requires extensive training in diverse data
Parameter	**Deterministic Systems**	**Probabilistic Systems**

Algorithm choice	Rule-based predictors	Advanced techniques like neural networks, regression algorithms
Quality engineering practices	Standard practices	Customized to suit the probabilistic nature
Behavior in response to input	Fixed, follows specific guidelines	Adapts based on patterns in data
Response when no suitable match is found	As defined by the business rule	Seeks additional information from the user or as defined by the business rule

Table 3.1: *Comparison of Deterministic and Probabilistic Systems*

Challenges and considerations in evaluating the quality of probabilistic systems

We have grasped the fundamental distinctions between deterministic and probabilistic systems in our study of system behaviors. Deterministic systems operate based on predefined rules, consistently yielding the same output for a given input. In contrast, probabilistic systems incorporate elements of randomness and probability, resulting in varying outputs for the same input. Consequently, testing probabilistic systems poses unique challenges when attempting to assess their quality and reliability.

Now, let us delve into the testing process for deterministic systems. Given that these systems adhere to predetermined rules, their testing methodology is based on the traditional Quality Engineering process, as outlined in **Chapter 1, Quality Engineering in the Era of AI**. This well-established approach serves as a comprehensive framework for effectively evaluating the performance and accuracy of deterministic systems, ensuring their adherence to the specified requirements and expected outcomes.

Evaluating the quality of deterministic systems takes into consideration the following process:

- Understand the functionality of the application under Test

    o Analyze system requirements and specifications

    o Ensure a thorough understanding of behavior and expected outputs

- Create a test design by generating the test cases

    o Cover all functionalities and scenarios to be evaluated

- o   Ensure 100% test coverage
- Identify and provision the test data needed for test cases:
  - o   Gather and organize necessary input data for each test case
  - o   Ensure all possible scenarios are covered
- Generate test scripts for automated test execution
  - o   Write scripts for the chosen test automation tool
  - o   Design scripts to efficiently execute test cases and capture results
- Execute the test cases and capture the test results:
  - o   Test scripts using the test automation tool
  - o   Monitor test execution and record results for each test case
- Generate test reports and raise defects for failed test cases:
  - o   Analyze test results and identify deviations from expected behavior
  - o   Report defects for further investigation and resolution.

Having understood the well-accepted approach to evaluating deterministic systems, let us delve into the challenges in evaluating probabilistic systems. Probabilistic systems, which rely heavily on Artificial Intelligence (AI) and Machine Learning (ML), present several obstacles when assessing their quality.

Dependency on Data Quality

High-quality data is essential for AI models but can be challenging to obtain.
AI and machine learning systems depend on clean, complete, and reliable data, but data flaws can impair their performance:

- **Incomplete data**: Missing or insufficient data limits model accuracy. **Example**: A virtual assistant may perform poorly if its training data needs the keywords to understand user questions.

- **Inconsistent data**: Variations in data formats lead to processing issues. **Example**: Different date formats (DDMMYY vs. MMDDYYYY) in user inputs can confuse a virtual assistant and result in incorrect responses.

- **Duplicate data**: Redundant entries reduce model efficiency. **Example**: Similar questions worded differently can clutter the training dataset of a virtual assistant.

- **Biased data**: Uneven representation of data skews outcomes. **Example**: A virtual assistant trained mainly on positive feedback may need to respond more effectively to negative customer reviews.

- **Structured vs. unstructured data**: Handling unstructured data remains challenging. **Example**: A virtual assistant might need help to analyze and categorize open-ended data, such as social media posts or customer reviews

Absence of Predicted Outcomes (Ground Truth)

Some AI models rely on dynamic outcomes rather than predefined answers. While classification models have known results, unsupervised learning approaches produce variable outcomes depending on input data. **Example**: In customer segmentation using clustering algorithms, the number of segments and their characteristics change based on the input, making it difficult to validate the results.

Outcomes Are Not Binary

Probabilistic systems give predictions with confidence scores, not just 'yes' or 'no' answers. These systems predict outcomes and the probability of correctness, which complicates their evaluation. **Example**: An AI system analyzing manufacturing defects might predict a design defect with 82% confidence. This implies an 18% chance that the root cause lies elsewhere, demanding a nuanced approach to assessing accuracy beyond binary judgments.

Test Coverage Challenges

Testing AI systems is more complex than testing rule-based systems. Unlike deterministic systems, which follow specific rules, probabilistic models rely on data patterns, making it hard to cover every scenario through testing.

- **Deterministic systems**: Test cases map directly to functionalities, ensuring comprehensive coverage and predictable outcomes. Example: All potential input-output combinations can be tested systematically.
- **Probabilistic systems**: Data diversity during training impacts accuracy, making full test coverage difficult. **Example**: A virtual assistant trained without exposure to diverse accents or phrasing may perform poorly when encountering such inputs

Testing probabilistic models often requires iterative methods like cross-validation and continuous monitoring to capture variations and outliers over time.

Evaluation Using Statistical Accuracy

Statistical accuracy alone isn't enough to assess AI models. While statistical accuracy provides insights during unit testing, it may not reflect how well the system performs in real-world conditions. **Example**: A virtual assistant might score high on statistical accuracy but need help in functional testing due to context-specific or cultural nuances missed during training.

Evaluating the performance of probabilistic systems requires new testing strategies. Deterministic systems follow predefined rules, ensuring consistent outputs. In contrast, probabilistic systems, such as those used in AI and ML, introduce randomness, leading to variable results for the same input. These differences make traditional quality engineering practices insufficient for assessing probabilistic models. Adapting testing frameworks for probabilistic systems involves strategies like data quality assessment, diverse test coverage, and continuous performance monitoring. By refining testing processes and incorporating adaptive methods, we can improve the evaluation and reliability of AI-powered virtual assistants and other probabilistic applications.

Adopting quality engineering practices for assessing the reliability and performance of probabilistic AI system

In the previous section, we discussed the challenges in evaluating the quality of probabilistic AI systems. This section provides an overview of how quality engineering practices can be adapted to effectively evaluate the various components of AI and ML applications, including unit testing, functional testing, and API interactions, while discussing optimization techniques for structured data testing.

Unit Testing of ML/AL Components

Unit testing is a crucial aspect of assessing the quality of ML and AI components. A layered approach is typically employed to validate the model using various statistical tools. One possible approach to unit testing involves validating the model at different levels, ensuring that each component performs as expected.

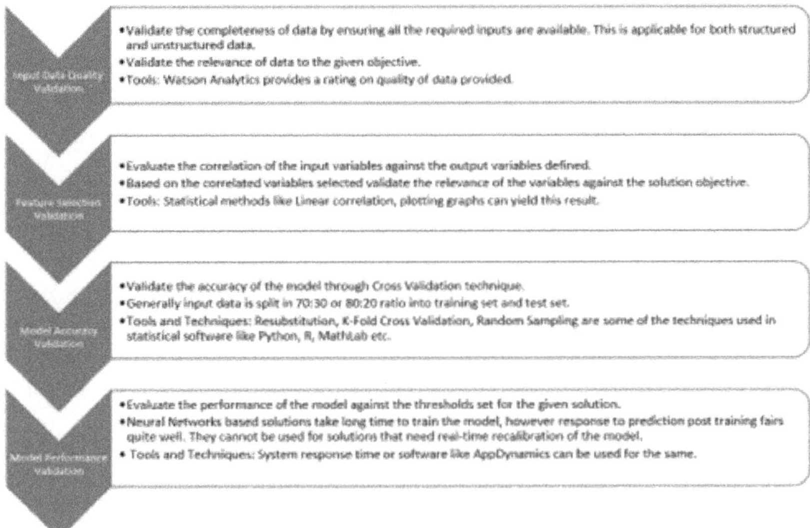

Figure 3.1: *A sample unit test approach*

Function Testing an ML/AI application

Machine Learning and Artificial Intelligence applications should be functionally tested at different layers. These layers should be identified based on the various architectural components of the application.

As discussed earlier, these are the following layers of ML/AI applications:

- User Interface
- ML/AI component
- API architecture that integrates the above components.

User Interface Testing

A variety of open-source and proprietary software is available for user interface testing. Selenium-based solutions are particularly popular due to their ease of use and the availability of expertise. Many tools also offer script-less solutions for testing user interfaces supported by Selenium. These tools can optimize and automate testing across both web and mobile interfaces. For example, when testing the user interface of a chatbot, tools like Selenium can be used to verify that the chat window appears correctly on different devices and browsers, that user inputs are processed correctly, and that the chatbot provides appropriate responses based on the user's query.

ML/AI Components

Testing of ML/AI components has been significantly constrained to Unit Testing due to the need to be frequently validated to check the quality of the model. There are multiple statistical methods to evaluate the same at unit test methods like R Squared, Adjusted R Squared, F-test, etc. The challenge is to find an approach to test these models at the functional testing level. We will discuss some options available to perform functional testing of ML/AI models based on the category. Testing each of the given categories of will need different approaches. We will touch on some of these categories and provide an approach to testing them.

For instance, when testing a supervised learning model for predicting customer churn, a functional testing approach may involve using real-world data to validate the model's predictions. This could involve comparing the model's predictions to actual customer churn data and assessing the model's accuracy, precision, and recall.

Model-based Testing Approach for Test Design and Coverage

Machine Learning solutions can be built using structured or unstructured data in all the above categories of ML/AI solutions. Identifying different test scenarios could be challenging to test these solutions. A model-based testing approach, like the Combinatorial Test Design (CTD), can be adopted to identify tests that cover all the possible transactions of an application or system. Combinatorial Test Design (CTD) is a proven technique that uses mathematical modelling to identify the points of variation in the test set and generate test scenarios with 100% test coverage. You can refer to the white paper given below to understand the approach. The key to identifying the points of variations for creating the CTD model is to know the features selected for the ML model creation. These features could be direct or indirect. A tester needs to know the final set of direct or derived features selected for the model to identify the points of variations.

To create a Combinatorial Test Design (CTD) model for this problem, we must first identify the points of variation based on the features selected for creating the model. Let us assume the following features were selected:

- Number of testers
- Complexity of the project

- Testing methodology
- Historical defect rate

To create a CTD model, we will consider each feature as a point of variation and define the possible values for each feature. For example:

- Number of testers: {5, 10, 15, 20}
- Complexity of the project: {Low, Medium, High}
- Testing methodology: {Manual, Automated, Hybrid}
- Historical defect rate: {Low, Medium, High}

Now, we can create a CTD model using these points of variation and their possible values:

Number of testers	Complexity of the project	Testing methodology	Historical defect rate
0 to 5	Low	Manual	Low
6 to 20	Medium	Automated	Medium
21 to 50	High	Hybrid	High
50 to 100			
Above 100			

Table 3.2: Sample CDT model values

The CTD model will generate various test scenarios with combinations of these features, ensuring 100% test coverage. By using pair-wise testing or other coverage criteria, we can reduce the number of test scenarios while maintaining high coverage. This CTD model can then guide the testing process, ensuring that the regression model is tested thoroughly across different combinations of features. While there are few test modelling tools available in the market, IBM's Haifa Research Labs has developed an approach to use Combinatorial Test Design to identify the scenario needed to test these solutions.

Testing API interactions within the application

The functional testing team will only be visible to some low-level software components. The underlying API structure plays a significant role in integrating the solution. Testing the APIs before or during integration will eliminate the defects delivered for the integration phase.

There are multiple tools available in the industry that can perform API testing. The developers use open-source solutions like Postman to validate the APIs during the unit testing phase. Other solutions to automate the API testing include Tricentis TOSCA, MicroFocus UFT, and IBM's IGNITE Quality Platform.

In summary, adopting quality engineering practices to assess the reliability and performance of probabilistic AI systems involves addressing the unique challenges posed by these systems. Organizations can ensure that their AI and ML applications perform reliably and accurately by focusing on unit testing, functional testing and API interactions and optimizing test scenarios for structured data testing. As AI technology advances, developing and refining evaluation methodologies that effectively assess quality is crucial.

Statistical analysis techniques for evaluating probabilistic outputs

In the previous section, we have already discussed the testing approach to evaluate probabilistic AI systems at each component level. This section will explore statistical analysis techniques that can be employed to evaluate the performance and reliability of AI and ML systems, focusing on supervised learning for classification and regression solutions and unsupervised learning. The discussion will include an introduction to confusion matrices, receiver operating characteristic (ROC) curves, and other relevant statistical tools.

Supervised Learning – Classification solutions

Classification based solutions are trained to predict a predefined set of outcome values. Considering that the outcome values are predefined, we have a definite scope to test the quality of the models. A confusion matrix summarizes the prediction results of the given classification problem.

What is a Confusion Matrix?

As per definition, "the confusion matrix shows how your classification model is confused when it makes predictions.". As per Data School, "A confusion matrix is a table that is often used to describe the performance of a classification model (or "classifier") on a set of test data for which the true values are known." To simplify, the confusion matrix summarizes correct and incorrect predictions with count values and is broken down by predefined outcome values.

Let us consider a two-class problem where the outcome of the prediction is limited to only two values. This gives us the following confusion matrix.

Description	Outcome 1		Outcome 2	
	Expected Outcome	Unexpected Outcome	Expected Outcome	Unexpected Outcome
Event	True-posi	False-negative	True-positive	False-negative
No-Event	False-posi-tive	True-negative	False-positive	True-negative

Table 3.3: Confusion Matrix

Let us take an example of identifying spam emails in your inbox. There can be only two categories: either an email is SPAM or not. A typical confusion matrix will be represented as below:

Description	Email is identified as SPAM	Email is not identified as SPAM
Email is a SPAM	True-positive	False-negative
Email is not a SPAM	False-positive	True-negative

Table 3.4: Confusion Matrix – SPAM Emails

Accuracy is computed as (TP + TN) / (TP + TN + FP + FN).
Precision is computed as TP / (TP + FP)
Recall is computed as TP / (TP + FN)

How can confusion matrix output be interpreted using the Receiver Operating Characteristic curve?

The receiver Operation Characteristic (ROC) curve is a probability curve used to measure the performance of the classification problem at various threshold levels. The ROC curve is created by plotting the actual positive rate (TPR) against the false positive rate (FPR) at various threshold settings.

True Positive Rate (TPR) = TP / (TP + FN)
False Positive Rate (FPR) = FP / (FP + TN)

The Area Under the Curve (AUC) analysis at different threshold values is analyzed to identify the optimal threshold for classification solutions. During testing, the tester should validate the AUC value at different thresholds and validate with client requirements to identify the optimal threshold for finalizing the model.

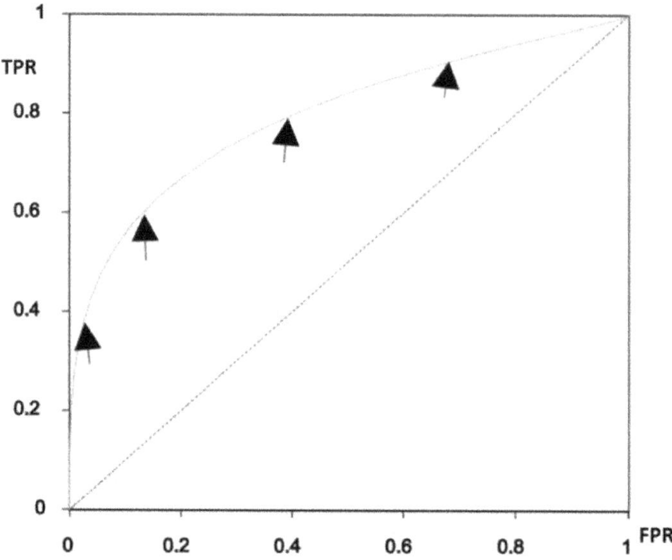

Figure 3.2: A representative area under the curve graph

Supervised Learning – Regression Solutions

Regression/Predictive solutions predict continuous valued output. These solutions represent the co-relationship between the input variables and predicted output values. These models are tested using statistical methods like r-squared or adjusted r-squared analysis during the unit testing level.

- Functional testing of such models could be used through statistical analysis.

- Pick up a set of test data that has yet to be used as part of the Training set or Test set during the model creation and unit testing process.

- Perform testing for the Function Test data set and validate the variance between actual and predicted values.

- Compute the Standard deviation and decide the accuracy based on an acceptable threshold.

- Other statistical tools are available to validate the quality of the model as well.

Let us take an example of a regression problem where we will predict how many new defects will be raised during the Functional Test phase. There can be multiple algorithms that can provide a suitable solution for this problem. In this example, we can use algorithms like Lasso, Ridge, Random Forest, or an ensemble of Random

Forest and Ridge to make the prediction. To evaluate the accuracy, we need to use the Test set in the Functional Test phase to validate the outcome. A simple variance comparison can give the accuracy of the outcome. The graph compares the variance in prediction outcome versus the actual across the project delivery in the functional testing phase. We have compared four models to select the most suitable solution. The solution with the slightest variance was selected for production deployment.

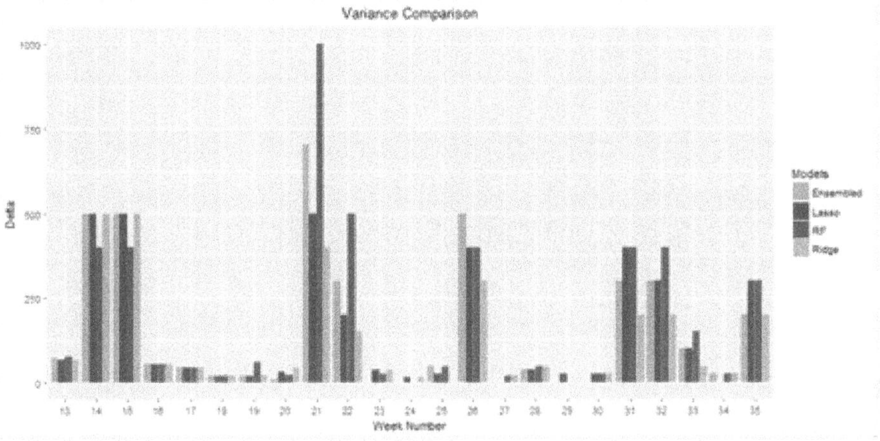

Figure 3.3: *A sample variance comparison graph using different regression models*

The graph represents the actual values on the y-axis at 0, and the prediction variance is on the y-axis. Based on variance analysis, Ridge, the algorithm has the slightest variance and should be selected as the most suitable model. Though this represents the selection of a model among multiple solutions, in a functional test, each solution's variance analysis can provide a good insight into the quality of the model.

- A good guideline would be to verify if the prediction variance against the actual is consistent and without any outliers.

- Similar statistical analytics can provide a suitable approach to validate the outcome of a regression model.

Unsupervised Learning

Unsupervised learning is used to identify various clusters in the input data. No expected result can be validated as the outcome of the prediction. In this case, only unit testing is possible, and the outcome is an inference of the input data provided. Cluster models are created using various clustering algorithms. To test these solutions, for each test data point not available in the training set, find out the proximity of the data point from the centroid of each cluster and manually predict the cluster that this data point belongs to. Validate the manual prediction with the model prediction and decide if the Test is successful. For example, in an unsupervised learning problem clustering customer data based on purchasing behavior, the model's performance could be assessed by examining the proximity of data points from the centroid of each cluster. The tester could manually predict the cluster a data point belongs to and validate this prediction against the model's prediction to determine if the Test is successful. Any unsupervised learning solution will require the data scientist to build the evaluation framework while developing the AI/ML model. This will allow the tester to visualize the solution and test it better.

In addition to the above approach, after creating the confusion matrix, some of the following methods can be used to validate the results:

- **Rand Measure**: The Rand index (RI) computes how similar the clusters (returned by the clustering algorithm) are to the benchmark classifications. Rand index measures the percentage of correct decisions made by the model.

$$RI = (TP + TN) / (TP + TN + FP + FN)$$

- **Dice-Index**: The Dice symmetric measure doubles TP's weight while ignoring TN. This approach is used for image segmentation for comparing the performance of algorithms.

$$DSC = (2 * TP) / (2TP + FP + FN)$$

- ROC curve explained in supervised classification can also be used to identify the optimal threshold at which the ML model provides the most suitable prediction to the client.

In summary, various statistical analysis techniques can be employed to effectively evaluate the performance and reliability of AI and ML systems with probabilistic outputs. These techniques include confusion matrices, receiver operating characteristic curves for classification solutions, and various error metrics for regression solutions. Custom evaluation frameworks may be necessary to assess the model's performance in unsupervised learning. By leveraging these statistical tools and techniques, organizations can ensure the reliability and accuracy of their AI and ML systems, leading to more informed decision-making and better overall performance.

Conclusion

In this chapter, we understood the paradigm shift required for evaluating probabilistic AI systems instead of deterministic systems. The chapter began by exploring the differences between deterministic and probabilistic AI systems, highlighting the unique challenges that probabilistic systems pose regarding quality evaluation.

We discussed the challenges and considerations in evaluating the quality of probabilistic systems, such as the absence of predetermined outputs, non-binary representation of outcomes, and the disparity between statistical and real-time predictions. This discussion provided an understanding of the need to adapt quality engineering practices better to assess the reliability and performance of probabilistic AI systems. It then provided an overview of the different approaches to adapting quality engineering practices for probabilistic AI systems, focusing on unit testing, functional testing, and API interactions. It also covers optimization techniques for structured data testing, particularly emphasizing using Combinatorial Test Design (CTD) to identify test scenarios. Finally, the chapter delved into statistical analysis techniques for evaluating probabilistic outputs. It covers various methods for assessing the performance of supervised learning models in classification and regression problems and the challenges involved in evaluating unsupervised learning models. The chapter concluded by emphasizing the importance of leveraging these statistical tools and techniques to ensure the reliability and accuracy of AI and ML systems, ultimately leading to more informed decision-making and better overall performance.

In the next chapter, we will delve deeper into the various elements that constitute AI systems, such as machine learning models, data pipelines, and algorithms. We will examine the different quality evaluation methods for each of these components, equipping you with the knowledge to assess their performance. Furthermore, we will explore various approaches for identifying and addressing quality issues in AI system components, ensuring that you can effectively optimize and maintain the overall performance of your AI systems. This chapter will provide you with a comprehensive understanding of the intricacies involved in evaluating and enhancing AI systems, setting the stage for further exploration in the world of artificial intelligence.

Exercise: Test Your Understanding

Answer the following questions and test your understanding of learning from Chapter 3:

Q. 1. Which of the following is a characteristic of deterministic applications?

    A. Outcomes are determined based on statistical probabilities

    B. The behavior of these systems is less predictable due to complex computations

    C. Inputs directly influence the decisions made by the application

    D. Requires extensive training on diverse data and many data points to identify patterns

Q. 2. What is a key characteristic of probabilistic systems?

    A. Outcomes are predefined based on specific business rules or conditions

    B. The behavior and results of the application are predictable and consistent

    C. Outcomes are determined based on statistical probabilities

    D. Deterministic systems are standard in traditional business applications

Q. 3. In the context of probabilistic systems, achieving full test coverage is challenging because:

    A. It is easy to account for every variation, pattern, or outlier within the input data

    B. Data quality, consistency, and bias do not complicate the evaluation process

    C. It is difficult to account for every variation, pattern, or outlier within the input data

    D. Probabilistic systems follow predefined rules

Q. 4. Which of the following is a challenge in evaluating probabilistic systems?

    A. Dependency on data quality

    B. Presence of predicted outcomes (Ground Truth)

    C. Test coverage is easy to achieve

    D. Evaluation using non-statistical accuracy

Q. 5. What is the purpose of a confusion matrix in evaluating classification models?

    A. To summarize the prediction results of the given classification problem

    B. To predict continuous valued output

    C. To identify various clusters in the input data

    D. To evaluate the performance of regression models.

Chapter 4

Evaluating Components of AI Systems

In our previous discussion, we emphasized the crucial role of validating the quality of AI systems. We explored the distinction between deterministic and probabilistic systems and examined various approaches to assess their quality. In this chapter, we will delve deeper into the different components of an AI system and how to evaluate the quality of each component. Additionally, we will address unique methods for identifying challenges in testing these components and offer strategies to tackle them.

By exploring user interfaces, back-end interfaces, integration layers, data storage layers and machine learning components, quality engineers will be equipped with the knowledge required to evaluate and optimize AI systems effectively. This chapter serves as a foundation for understanding the structure and functionality of AI systems and provides insights into the various elements that contribute to their overall performance.

In this chapter, we will discuss the following topics:

- The different components of the AI Systems and how they interact with each other.
- The quality evaluation process for each of the components.
- Challenges in evaluating the quality of AI systems will be discussed as well.

Understanding the different components of AI Systems

AI systems share similarities with modern software applications, as both consist of three main components: a User Interface for user interaction, a Back-end Interface housing the solution's business logic and an Integration Layer that connects the User Interface with the Back-end Interface. Furthermore, a Data Storage Layer exists for preserving data.

Let us dissect these components further (**Fig. 4.1**)

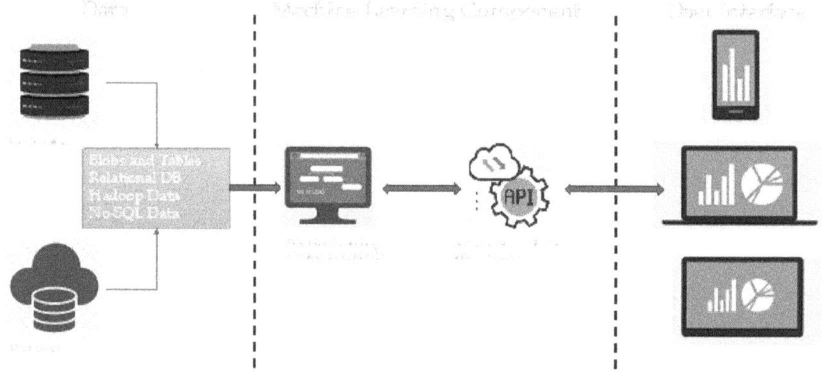

Figure 4.1: *Breakdown of components in AI Systems*

Data: The Cornerstone of AI Systems

Data is the most critical component of AI systems. Without good quality of data, the output of an AI system cannot be predictable. Understanding the characteristics of data in the context of AI system will provide deeper understanding in generating a strategy to evaluate the quality. Let us start by categorizing the data based on its representation. Data is the bedrock of any AI system. Ensuring high-quality data and proper management are paramount to the system's success.

First, we need to comprehend the data characteristics in AI systems, which can be categorized based on representation:

- Structured Data can be identified based on data type, format, length, and structure. For example, in India, credit card numbers in a banking application are categorized as numeric data types with a standard length of 16 digits.

- Unstructured Data is a combination of varying data types, format and Length. Generally freeform data is defined this this format. For example, images, audio files, videos and unstructured text are unstructured data.

Data can also be classified according to modalities, which denote the different data formats used for analysis. Some common data modalities in AI systems include:

- Time-series data is collected over time and represents the data changes over a period. For example, fluctuations in loan interest rates within a banking application over a decade.

- Text data: This includes documents, articles and unstructured text from emails or social media posts.

- Audio data: This captures sounds, speech and music in various audio file formats, such as .mpeg, .mp3, .wmv and .mov.

- Image data: Comprising photographs, images, and visual information. There are a wide range of data formats supporting images like .jpeg, .png etc.

- Video data encompasses moving images and their visual representations

In AI-powered applications, data usage varies based on the specific application. We will discuss the different contexts in which data is utilized:

- Production Dataset: This complete dataset, often consisting of historical data gathered over time, is used to develop a solution for a problem. For example, in defect analytics, all defects collected over several years form the production dataset.

- Training Dataset: A subset of the production dataset is employed to create the solution. The patterns in this dataset train the machine learning component of the AI application.

- Cross Validation/Testing Dataset: This dataset comprises the remaining portion of the production dataset not used for training the machine learning solution. It serves to validate or test the quality of the machine learning component and the AI application

During the AI solution development lifecycle, the production dataset is divided into training and cross-validation/testing datasets. Typical split ratios are 80%:20% or 90%:10% for training and testing datasets, respectively. The split ratio is determined based on the need for more training data versus test data.

With a solid understanding of data characteristics, we can now explore the data storage environments used for application development and testing:

- On-Premises Environments: Data is stored on private servers with access restricted to authorized users. The data is housed in secure data centres dedicated to the organization utilizing them.

- Cloud Environments: Data is stored on shared servers with secure access granted to authorized users. Cloud storage can also be provided on public domains.

User Interface

To use the capability developed for any application, an User Interface is needed to interact with ease. User interface provides the ability to interact with the system without delving deeper into technical components of the applications. The user interface is the mode to access the functionality of the application. This layer provides the user access to utilize the features of the application. The user interacts at a higher abstraction layer of the application.

In modern day systems, user interfaces are made available through different modes.

- Web Interface provides access to interact with the application using a web browser. This was the most used interface before widespread mobile use.

- Mobile Interface provides access to the user using a mobile application or through a mobile browser.

There are a wide range of technologies available to develop these user interfaces. In the context of AI systems, user interfaces provide the mode to represent the outcome of the application.

The representation of the outcome can be:

- Response to questions in a Chatbot application.

- A predicted outcome of a machine learning solution.

- Visualizations in data analysis tools in graphical representation.

- Providing recommendations in recommendation systems.

- Actionable insights derived from complex algorithms.

Integration layer using API interfaces

Application Programming Interfaces (API's) is the application's integration layer. This layer componentizes the application into smaller functions and provides a set of rules and protocols to communicate with other APIs or components of the application. API provides the ability to componentizing the entire applications into technical components. These components interact using a set of rules and protocols within and outside the scope of the application. Let's understand the API layer in detail.

There are different types of APIs:

- Web APIs (or HTTP APIs) can be accessed over the internet using HTTP/ HTTPS protocols. They enable communication between different web services.

- Library APIs provide specifications to programming languages and provide sets of functions or methods to be used in the code by the developers

- Operating System APIs allow applications to interact with the operating system. For example, Windows API, POSIX for Unix-like systems, etc.

- Hardware APIs provide interfaces for hardware components, like those used in computer graphics, sound cards, etc.

In AI systems, APIs communicate between machine learning and user interface components. They can also trigger tasks as a follow-up to the predicted outcome. In the context of AI systems, APIs are the mode of communication between machine learning and user interface components.

AI and Machine Learning (ML) Component

In Artificial Intelligence-based applications, these Machine Learning components are the soul of the entire application. They provide the AI capability to the application. Let us discuss these components in detail.

Let's delve deeper into these components. In the previous section, we examined the distinctions between machine learning and AI. Machine learning technology is required for constructing AI elements. Predicting outcomes is crucial in identifying the types of AI components.

The frequently used categories for Machine Learning are as follows:

Supervised Learning

Supervised Learning solutions are trained with the objective of obtaining a pre-defined outcome. When the solution is expecting a fixed set of pre-determined output values, a supervised learning approach is selected. When we plan to create a Chatbot solution using Watson Conversation service, the Intent and Entity values should be defined in the service and response for each of the same should also be defined. The learning algorithm will take these values to train the algorithm to look for the defined intent and entities. Another example is that the classification of defects based on their root cause falls under the category of Classification solutions. In this case, the categories of the root cases are pre-defined. At the same time, predicting the inflow of defects throughout the test life cycle is categorized as a Regression solution. This solution predicts the continuous-valued output (in the flow of defects) within the scope defined for the project or release. A further illustration involves the categorization of defects according to their root causes, which falls under the Classification solutions category. In this scenario, the root cause categories are predetermined. Simultaneously, forecasting the influx of defects during the testing life cycle is classified as a Regression solution. This approach anticipates the continuous-valued output (in terms of defect flow) within the boundaries established for the project or release. There are a few variations in supervised learning-based solutions.

The frequently used solutions are given below:

- Classification based solutions are used to predict the outcome based on the input parameters. For example, identification of spam mails is based on this use case.

- Regression based solutions are used to predict the trend of the patterns based on historical data and influencing parameters. Forecasting the weather is one such example.

Unsupervised Learning

During daily conversations, having Chatbot like solutions that have been trained to identify pre-defined intents and entities may not be suitable. You would need a more dynamic approach to identify the various intents and entities without defining them. In these scenarios, Unsupervised Learning solutions are used. They allow the algorithms to determine the output clusters available in the input data. Identifying the product preferences of potential buyers based on their social network interaction is one of the scenarios where these approaches are used.

Some of variations of unsupervised learning-based solutions are:

- Clustering solutions are used to identify groups or clusters in the data. Use cases to create customer segmentation in e-commerce applications based on their browsing history, wish list and purchase history fall under this category.

- Dimension Reduction solutions are used to identify the features influencing decision making. Continuing with the e-commerce application, this solution can help in identifying the customer's buying pattern through identification of parameters influencing it.

Reinforcement Learning

With robotics gaining lots of prominence in the industry, a combination of Bots and AI based solutions are getting developed rapidly. To support such solutions, a dynamic programming method like Reinforcement Learning is needed. Such solutions will be dynamically adopted based on past learnings and reinforce the changes over a period. Robot control is one of the commonly used applications where reinforcement learning is applied.

There are variations to reinforcement learning based applications as well. They are:

- Model free solutions are used to identify the learn from system patterns without a model to reinforce the decision. For example, learning modules can be developed based on optimal policy defined to identify the next training module without a predefined model.

- Model based solution need a model in place to decide the next action to be taken. This approach is used in gaming solutions to reinforce the complexity level of the player.

A new set of AI applications uses generative transformation technology to generate content. These are categorized as Generative AI applications. We will be discussing these applications in detail in subsequent chapters.

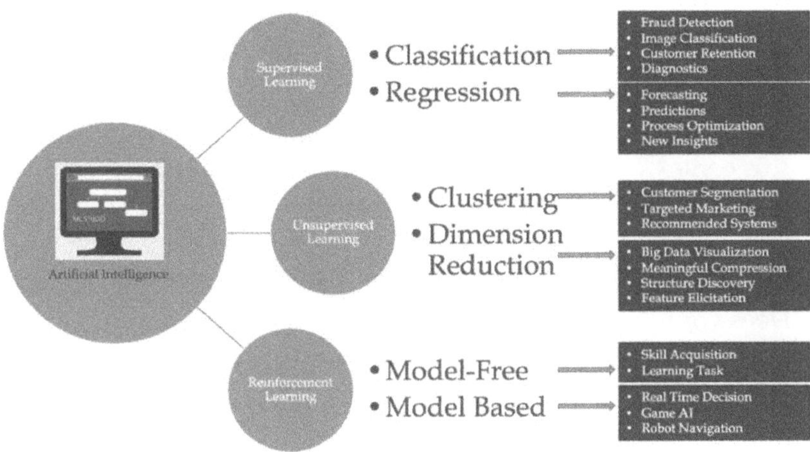

Figure 4.2: *Machine Learning solutions with examples*

Having a solid grasp of the fundamental components of an AI system is crucial in devising an effective quality evaluation strategy for these applications. This knowledge enables us to establish a comprehensive approach to assessing each component and facilitates the development of a holistic strategy encompassing the entire AI system. The following section will delve deeper into this topic and discuss the intricacies of creating such evaluation strategies. A novel group of AI applications employs generative transformation technology to produce content, falling under the category of Generative AI applications. We will explore these applications in greater depth in upcoming chapters.

In summary, understanding the essential building blocks of an AI system is vital for formulating an efficient quality assessment plan for these applications. This expertise allows us to devise a thorough method for evaluating each component and fosters the creation of a comprehensive strategy that covers the entire AI system. The subsequent section will further explore this subject and examine the complexities involved in developing such assessment strategies.

The Crucial Need for Quality Evaluation of AI System Components

After understanding the components and their characteristics of an AI system, we will now focus on evaluating the quality of these components. This section will define the key considerations that should be taken to evaluate the quality of these components. We will discuss the methods to evaluate the quality of these components in subsequent chapters.

Data Quality Assessment

In the previous section, we discussed the importance of data in the context of AI systems. Now, let us understand the key considerations for evaluating the quality of data. In this context, we should ask the following questions:

- How do you validate the quality of Training Data?
- Do all the business combinations sufficiently represent in training data?
- Does your data consist of bias towards certain data combinations?
- How will you test when the training data is not available for validation?
- How will you replicate training data bias in test data?

We will start by answering the question "How do you validate the quality of Data". By the end of this book, all these questions will be thoroughly addressed.

Defining the Quality Metrics for Data

Now, let's define the quality metrics that are needed to validate the quality of data. These metrics are essential for ensuring that the data used in AI systems is reliable and accurate. In the context of ecommerce applications, the following metrics are particularly relevant:

- **Completeness**: This metric focuses on ensuring that all mandatory data elements are available in the desired format. For example, in an ecommerce application, customer details such as name, address, and email should be available in the format defined by the application.

- **Uniqueness**: This metric ensures that the data points available do not have any duplicates. In ecommerce applications, customer details should not have any duplicated entries. The combination of mandatory data fields needed to identify a customer should be unique.

- **Consistency**: This metric ensures that all the data elements for a given feature follow the same representation. This consistency is crucial for ensuring that the analysis of data is reliable. For example, the customer's order details in an ecommerce application should always be in the same format. If the application has chosen to use the dd/mm/yyyy format to represent date values, then every instance of the date value in the date field should adhere to this format.

- **Accuracy**: This metric defines the ability to identify the data point without any ambiguity based on its characteristics or description. In an ecommerce application, my past transactions should be accurately shown in my order history.

- **Timeliness**: This metric indicates the relevance of data at the time it is used. In an ecommerce application, cancelled orders do not add any value in the context of analyzing on-time delivery metrics for a seller.

- **Validity**: This metric indicates the validity of the data in the current context in which it is being used. In the above example of ecommerce applications, past deals provided by the application are no longer valid after the offer period ends.

All the above metrics are crucial for validating the quality of data. In the subsequent chapters, we will discuss different approaches to validate data based on these dimensions.

User Interface Assessment

We discussed how user interfaces provide the users of the AI Systems an abstraction layer to interpret and consume the data. Validating the quality of the user interfaces is performed in two perspectives.

- User Interfaces should meet the desired standards as prescribed by the developing organizations standards. The key aspects of validations are defined based on design standards defined by the organization developing these user interfaces. Some of the key aspects taken into consideration are,

    o All the elements defined in the user interface should be clearly visible to the user.

    o The UI elements should be consistent in terms of visuals, like size, design and color scheme.

    o User interfaces should follow accessibility standards that support the ease of use for differently abled users as well.

Example: In an e-commerce application, UI elements must adhere to design standards, ensuring elements are visible, consistent in visuals, and follow specified accessibility standards.

- Use the user interface to validate the functionality of the application. User interfaces are used to validate if the applications meet the requirements specification defined. It should be able to provide an interface to get the outcome and compare the same with the expected outcome.

Example: In an e-commerce application, the recommended products should be related to user's preferences and past browsing history.

Integration Layer validation using Application Programming Interface (API)

The application testing team will only have visibility to some low-level software components. The underlying Application Programming Interface (API) structure plays a significant role in integrating the solution. Testing the APIs before or during integration will eliminate the defects delivered for the integration phase. The complete specifications help to test APIs with proper business use cases. The specifications define the rules and requirements of how the program/module should interact with other systems in the application. Specifications on the method, data formats, protocols, and end-point definitions should be specified to evaluate the APIs. Based on this information, the quality evaluation of the APIs focuses on validating the adherence to these specifications. The application testing team typically has access to only a few low-level software components. The underlying Application Programming Interface (API) architecture is crucial for integrating the solution. Examining the APIs before or during integration helps to prevent defects from arising during the integration phase. Comprehensive specifications facilitate the testing of APIs with relevant business use cases. These specifications outline the rules and requirements for how the program or module should interact with other systems within the application. Details regarding the method, data formats, protocols, and endpoint definitions should be provided to assess the APIs effectively. Based on this information, the quality evaluation of the APIs primarily concentrates on verifying compliance with these specifications.
Validating the API layer involves:

- Defining specifications for APIs, including rules, data formats, protocols, and endpoint definitions. **Example**: In an e-commerce application, API specifications would outline how the ordering system interacts with the inventory management system, specifying data formats and communication protocols.

- Evaluating adherence to API specifications to ensure smooth integration. **Example**: Verifying that the communication between the ordering system and the inventory management system in an e-commerce application follows the specified API rules.

Artificial Intelligence/ Machine Learning

Component

AI or ML components are the core of AI infused systems. The quality of these components is critical dimension in evaluating the quality of these applications/systems. The quality of AI components needs to be evaluated in the following dimensions.

- **Accuracy of Prediction**: This dimension assesses the ability of the AI/ML component to predict the outcome correctly. Unlike deterministic systems, the accuracy of AI predictions is determined statistically. For example, in an e-commerce application, an AI component may predict customer preferences based on past behavior. The accuracy of these predictions is crucial for providing personalized recommendations to customers. In an e-commerce application, accurate prediction of customer preferences based on historical data is crucial for personalized recommendations.

- **Confidence of Prediction**: In probabilistic AI/ML systems, the confidence score indicates the level of certainty in the predicted outcome. This dimension measures the confidence level of the AI component in its predictions. For instance, an AI component may predict the likelihood of a customer purchasing a particular product. The confidence score provides insight into the reliability of this prediction. An e-commerce recommendation system may provide a confidence score, indicating the likelihood that a user will be interested in a particular product.

- **Response Time**: This dimension evaluates the time taken by the AI system to provide an outcome. In real-time applications, such as chatbots or recommendation engines, the response time plays a vital role in maintaining a seamless user experience. The AI component should be able to generate predictions or responses within an acceptable timeframe. In an e-commerce application, the response time of a product recommendation system is critical to providing a seamless user experience during browsing.

- **Consistency**: Consistency determines the ability of the AI system to provide the same outcome even for minor or trivial changes to the inputs. It reflects the stability and robustness of the AI component. For example, in a conversation solution, the user's behaviour cannot be constrained. The system should return the same predicted outcome irrespective of the length of the query as long as the context and content are same.

The need for quality evaluation of every component of an AI system is crucial to ensure its effectiveness and reliability. We can identify potential issues or flaws that may impact the system's performance by assessing the data quality, user interface, integration layer, and AI/ML components. Evaluating the data involves considering completeness, uniqueness, consistency, accuracy, timeliness, and validity metrics.

The user interface assessment focuses on meeting design standards and validating the application's functionality. Validating the integration layer using APIs helps ensure smooth integration and eliminates defects. Lastly, evaluating the AI/ML components involves assessing accuracy, confidence, response time, and consistency. By thoroughly evaluating each component, we can enhance AI systems' overall quality and performance. To summarize, the importance of conducting a quality assessment for each element of an AI system is critical to guarantee its efficiency and dependability. By examining the data quality, user interface, integration layer, and AI/ML components, we can detect potential problems or shortcomings that may influence the system's performance. Data evaluation entails considering metrics such as completeness, uniqueness, consistency, accuracy, timeliness, and validity. The user interface assessment emphasizes compliance with design standards and verification of the application's functionality. Validating the integration layer using APIs ensures seamless integration and reduces defects. Finally, evaluating the AI/ML components consists of examining accuracy, confidence, response time, and consistency. By meticulously assessing each component, we can improve the overall quality and performance of AI systems.

Navigating Unique Challenges in Evaluating the Quality of AI and ML Components

In this chapter, we have understood the components of AI and ML applications. The need to evaluate the quality of these components and the dimensions to be considered for quality assessment was also discussed.

Let us understand some of the key considerations to evaluate the quality of these components.

Challenges in Evaluating AI Systems

The evaluation of AI systems poses unique challenges, necessitating a nuanced approach to ensure accurate assessments. Here, we discuss some of these challenges and outline corresponding strategies to address them.

Complex Modalities of Data

The inherent complexity of data modalities, such as free-form text, audio, and visual data, requires a tailored evaluation approach. Building upon the dimensions defined earlier, the evaluation of these modalities must adapt to the specific characteristics of the application. **Example**: Consider a conversation system within an e-commerce application. When assessing free-text input, it becomes crucial to evaluate the semantic space, gauging the cohesiveness of the data and associated labels. For instance, training data used to relate queries on product orders should be organized in semantic space, ensuring accurate predictions by the system.

Generating Test Data for Complex Modalities

Creating test data for intricate modalities demands advanced machine learning solutions. Synthetic text data, for instance, requires linguistic models, while generating audio data may involve complex techniques such as Text to Speech synthesis and Video cloning. **Example**: In an e-commerce application, generating synthetic text data for product descriptions involves training linguistic models to create realistic and diverse text inputs. Similarly, utilizing Text to Speech synthesis for generating audio data ensures a comprehensive evaluation of the system's capabilities.

Validating Outcomes for Complex Modalities

The validation of outcomes in the realm of complex data modalities presents its own set of challenges. Solutions like visual comparisons, developed for browser compatibility testing in web application test automation, demonstrate the complexity of ensuring accurate assessments. **Example**: A visual comparison tool in an e-commerce application ensures the proper rendering of product images across different devices and browsers, contributing to the overall quality assessment of the AI system.

Lack of Availability of Expected Outcome

In certain scenarios, the dynamic nature of AI systems, especially in e-commerce applications, makes it challenging to establish a consistent expected outcome. Product recommendations based on user preferences, browsing behavior, and purchase history can change frequently, requiring an approach centered around anomaly identification for evaluation. **Example**: In an e-commerce setting, the absence of a static expected outcome for product recommendations necessitates a continuous evaluation strategy. Identifying anomalies, such as sudden shifts in user behavior, becomes a crucial aspect of assessing system quality.

Probabilistic Nature of AI Systems

The inherent probabilistic nature of AI systems introduces ambiguity in the matching process between predicted and expected outcomes. Instead of absolute matches or mismatches, evaluating the confidence score associated with predictions becomes imperative. **Example**: In an e-commerce application, where predicting user preferences is probabilistic, understanding the confidence score associated with each recommendation enhances the reliability of the system's outputs.

Evaluating the quality of AI and ML components involves navigating through intricate challenges. By addressing the unique characteristics of data modalities, employing sophisticated techniques for test data generation, and adapting validation approaches, a comprehensive evaluation framework can be established. Embracing the dynamic nature of AI systems and leveraging probabilistic assessments further enhances the accuracy of quality evaluations, ensuring robust performance in real-world applications.

Conclusion

This chapter has provided a comprehensive overview of the evaluation of components in AI systems. We began by emphasizing the importance of validating the quality of AI systems and discussed the distinctions between deterministic and probabilistic systems. The focus then shifted to a deeper exploration of the various components of AI systems, including user interfaces, back-end interfaces, integration layers, data storage layers, and machine learning components. A crucial aspect highlighted in this chapter is the significance of data, considering its various types, modalities, and usage contexts in AI applications. We also delved into the evaluation of user interfaces, emphasizing adherence to design standards and functional validation. The integration layer, utilizing APIs, was discussed in terms of specifications and adherence to ensure smooth system integration.

The heart of AI applications, the machine learning components, were dissected into categories such as supervised, unsupervised, and reinforcement learning. The dimensions for evaluating these components, including accuracy, confidence, response time, and consistency, were thoroughly examined. Furthermore, the chapter underscored the importance of quality evaluation for each component, considering metrics like completeness, uniqueness, consistency, accuracy, timeliness, and validity for data, adhering to design standards, and validating functionality for user interfaces. API specifications were outlined for the integration layer, and dimensions like accuracy, confidence, response time, and consistency were discussed for AI/ML components. The subsequent section delved into the challenges faced in evaluating AI and ML components, emphasizing the complexity of data modalities, the generation of test data, the validation of outcomes, the lack of an expected outcome, and the probabilistic nature of AI systems. Strategies were proposed to address these challenges, including tailored evaluation approaches, advanced machine learning solutions, and probabilistic assessments.

In the final part of the chapter, the focus shifted to the paradigm shift required for evaluating probabilistic AI systems compared to deterministic ones. The challenges and considerations specific to probabilistic systems were outlined, and various approaches, including unit testing, functional testing, API interactions, and statistical analysis techniques, were discussed to adapt quality engineering practices for these systems. This chapter lays the foundation for a holistic understanding of AI systems' components and their quality evaluation. It equips quality engineers with the knowledge required to assess each component effectively and emphasizes the need for a comprehensive strategy that encompasses the entire AI system. The subsequent chapters will further delve into the intricacies of creating evaluation strategies for these components, offering valuable insights for practitioners in the field.

In summary, you got an overview of assessing components in AI systems. We started by stressing the significance of verifying AI systems' quality and examining the differences between deterministic and probabilistic systems. We then delved deeper into the various elements of AI systems, including user interfaces, back-end interfaces, integration layers, data storage layers, and machine learning components. A vital aspect highlighted in this chapter is the importance of data, considering its different types, modalities, and usage contexts in AI applications. We also investigated the assessment of user interfaces, focusing on compliance with design standards and functional verification. The integration layer, utilizing APIs, was explored in terms of specifications and adherence to ensure seamless system integration. The core of AI applications, the machine learning components, were broken down into categories such as supervised, unsupervised, and reinforcement learning. The dimensions for evaluating these components, including accuracy, confidence, response time, and consistency, were comprehensively analyzed. Moreover, the chapter emphasized the need for quality assessment for each component, considering metrics like completeness, uniqueness, consistency, accuracy, timeliness, and validity for data, adherence to design standards, and functional verification for user interfaces. API specifications were detailed for the integration layer, and dimensions like accuracy, confidence, response time, and consistency were discussed for AI/ML components. The following section examined the challenges encountered when assessing AI and ML components, highlighting the complexity of data modalities, test data generation, outcome validation, the absence of an expected outcome, and the probabilistic nature of AI systems. Strategies were suggested to address these challenges, including customized evaluation approaches, advanced machine learning solutions, and probabilistic assessments. In the final part, the focus shifted to the paradigm change required for evaluating probabilistic AI systems compared to deterministic ones. The challenges and considerations specific to probabilistic systems were described, and various approaches, including unit testing, functional testing, API interactions, and statistical analysis techniques, were discussed to adapt quality engineering practices for these systems.

This chapter has set the foundation for a comprehensive understanding of AI systems' components and their quality assessment. It provides quality engineers with the necessary knowledge to effectively evaluate each component and emphasizes the need for an all-encompassing strategy that covers the entire AI system. Subsequent chapters will further explore the complexities of creating evaluation strategies for these components, offering valuable insights for professionals in the field.

Exercise: Test Your Understanding

Answer the following questions and test your understanding of learning from Chapter 4:

Q. 1. What are the different categories of data modalities discussed in the chapter, impacting the evaluation of AI systems?

    A.   Only structured data

    B.   Only unstructured data

    C.   Both structured and unstructured data

    D.   Only time-series data

Q. 2. In the context of AI systems, what is a key consideration when validating the quality of user interfaces for effective user experience?

    A.   Adherence to design standards

    B.   Data completeness

    C.   Integration with APIs

    D.   Backend interface optimization

Q. 3. What is the suggested approach for evaluating the integration layer using API interfaces in AI systems?

    A.   Ignoring specifications for smooth integration

    B.   Defining specifications for APIs and evaluating adherence

    C.   Focusing only on backend interfaces

    D.   Avoiding evaluation to save time

Q. 4. What are the critical dimensions discussed for evaluating the quality of AI components in the chapter?

    A.   Only accuracy of prediction

    B.   Only response time

    C.   Only response time

    D.   Only confidence of prediction

Q. 5. What are some of the challenges discussed in evaluating AI systems, especially those related to data modalities and the probabilistic nature of AI systems?

    A.   Only challenges related to data modalities

    B.   Only challenges related to the lack of availability of expected outcomes

    C.   Both challenges related to data modalities and the lack of availability of expected outcomes

    D.   Only challenges related to structured data

$\mathrm{Chapter}\ 5$

Customizing Quality Engineering Practices for AI

In the preceding chapter, we examined the components of AI systems and the importance of verifying their quality. We also explored the distinct challenges and methods to overcome them in the context of AI systems.

Now, let's discuss how quality engineering practices must be tailored to accommodate the evaluation of AI systems. We will investigate how conventional QE practices can be applied to AI systems and delve into AI-specific quality metrics necessary to achieve the objectives of validating AI systems. Additionally, we will address the regulatory compliance requirements needed to attain a comprehensive QE solution for these systems.

In this chapter, we will discuss the following topics:

- Adapting traditional quality engineering practices for AI systems
- Defining AI-specific quality metrics and objectives
- Incorporating AI-specific testing techniques
- Ensuring regulatory compliance in AI-driven solutions

Refining conventional quality engineering approaches for AI systems

AI systems can be as simple as a chat bot or complex systems like assisting large, connected transactions of a system. Testing AI systems will require evaluating the quality of different components of these systems. Firstly, let us understand assessing the quality of traditional AI system components, such as the User Interfaces and Integration layers. Further as we progress through following chapters, we will understand the evaluation of Data and AI components.

Let's look at a snapshot of how AI infused applications will be tested. We will discuss each of the aspects in detail (**Fig. 5.1**)

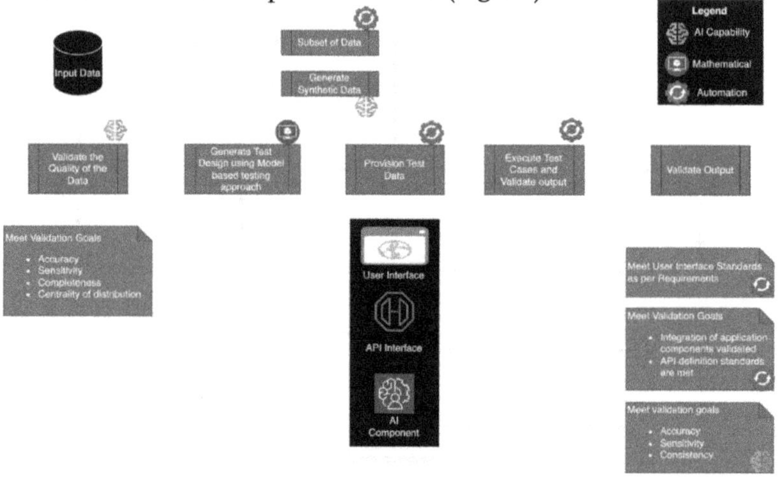

Figure 5.1: *AI infused application testing*

User Interface

Modern systems employ web or mobile interfaces to display the outcomes of any system. The representation of AI systems is not much different from traditional deterministic systems:

- The methods of utilizing user interfaces to assess AI systems' quality involve various validation modes. Manual Validation requires a tester to ensure that the outcome adheres to functional and user interface standards as defined for the application under test. This process involves comparing the outcome presented on the UI based on the input provided with the expected results defined in the test case and determining the test's success or failure.

- For instance, in an e-commerce application, the order confirmation is validated based on the provided confirmation message. Additionally, the confirmed order's availability in the user's order list serves as extra validation. This validation is performed manually by the tester without any intervention from tools.

- Automated Validation is carried out by test automation tools that follow a set of instructions. These tools are programmed to perform tasks on behalf of the tester. These instructions also account for the comparison of test results with expected outcomes and determine the test case's success or failure based on this comparison.

- Consider the ecommerce application example again. Here, the entire test workflow can be executed automatically using a test automation tool.

Let us look at some widely used automation tools in the industry. These tools or products are categorized based on the licensing mode defined by the product owner:

- Open-Source products or software come with the code and can be customized by users. Tools like Selenium, Robot Framework, etc., are available for users to download for free or at minimal cost and can be adapted to suit the application's testing needs. Commercial Off-The-Shelf (COTS) products are ready-made for purchase, lease, or subscription by users. COTS products like Tricentis TOSCA, IBM RFT, Microfocus UFT, etc., are available for automating test execution. They provide the ability to generate test scripts and map web or mobile application objects to execute tests automatically.

In the context of testing AI systems, we will discuss the customizations required for testing these probabilistic systems in the subsequent sections of this chapter.

Integration layer using API interfaces

Application Programming Interfaces (API) were discussed in the previous chapter. APIs need to be tested in the context of AI-based applications. Let us look at some basics of testing API interfaces.

Some applications of APIs in AI systems:

- All AI components are exposed as APIs to be consumed by other components of AI systems. In virtual assistants, chatbot modules like Watson Assistant, Azure LUIS, Google Assistant, etc., are exposed as APIs.

- Apart from AI modules or components, there are other components that interact with each other. These components are also exposed as APIs. In virtual assistants, besides chatbot modules, there may be modules triggered based on user queries. These modules perform specific activities such as filling out a form, reserving a ticket, etc., automatically.

In the context of AI systems, APIs are used to facilitate communication between AI or machine learning modules, other non-AI modules and user interface components. In the coming sections, we will discuss the process of API testing:

Understanding API Documentation

API documentation should include information on API specification, output format, and functionality of the API.
API Specifications provide the design and build method used to develop the APIs.

- OpenAPI/Swagger is a widely adopted specification for designing, building, documenting and consuming RESTful APIs. Many cloud applications use this specification.

- RAML (RESTful API Modeling Language): A YAML-based language for designing and documenting RESTful APIs.

- GraphQL: A query language and runtime for APIs that enables clients to request specific data and reduce over-fetching.

- gRPC: A high-performance, open-source framework for building remote procedure call (RPC) APIs.

Output format is essential to interpret the functionality of the modules exposed through APIs.
Few examples of output formats in APIs include:

- JSON (JavaScript Object Notation) is a lightweight data interchange format that is easy to read and write and easy for IT systems to parse and generate.

- XML (eXtensible Markup Language) is a markup language that defines rules for encoding documents in a format readable by both quality engineers and IT systems.

- CSV (Comma-Separated Values) is a simple file format that stores tabular data in plain text, with values separated by commas.

- YAML (YAML Ain't Markup Language) is a data serialization format used for configuration files and data exchange between languages, and it is human-readable.

- Protocol Buffers is a language-agnostic binary serialization format developed by Google. This format is considered efficient, extensible, and used for high-performance communication between systems.

Functionality of module/component exposed as APIs

APIs serve as a method to expose the modules/components that are part of AI systems. The functional specifications of the components are exposed as output of the APIs in the desired format. The module's functionality defines its purpose and contribution to the AI system.

For instance, in a voice-based virtual assistant, there are multiple modules like Chatbot module, Speech to Text, Text to Speech conversion modules, among others. Each of these modules performs a specific task, and its output is exposed as an API.

Design the Test for the APIs

During the design phase, the API specification, functionality, input format, output format, and expected results must be clearly defined. Based on this information, test cases need to be created. The test cases should define positive and negative test scenarios and cover boundary conditions for testing.

In testing a virtual assistants Chatbot module, the test cases need to be clearly defined.

- The input can accept text, audio, or visual input, etc. Let's consider the input to the chatbot as a text with the question: "How is the weather at Bangalore, India today?"

- The type of specification the API is developed in, such as YAML/ Swagger.

- The output format of this module could be JSON.

- The expected results are the response expected from the chatbot system. In this example, the expected result could be "It's a cloudy day with 80% chances of thundershower.

Execute the APIs

The test cases created in the design phase need to be executed. They can be executed programmatically as part of a code that triggers the APIs or can be tested independently using tools like Postman, SOAPUI, Jenkins, etc.

Validate the output of the API:

Validate the output of the API against the expected results defined in the test cases. If the API output matches the expected output, the test case is considered as pass.

Otherwise, it is considered a failure.

In the example of a virtual assistant mentioned previously, if the API has executed successfully with a return code of 200 and the response is the same as the expected output, then the test case is considered as pass.

This section has emphasized the adaptability of traditional quality engineering methods for testing AI-integrated systems. The subsequent discussion will explore various quality metrics and explain how customizing traditional QE approaches can enhance AI system testing effectiveness. The combination of established practices with emerging AI technologies propels quality engineering into a new era of precision and adaptability.

Define AI specific quality metrics and objectives

Before diving into the adaptation of quality engineering processes for assessing AI-integrated applications, it's important to identify the primary evaluation metrics. These metrics play a crucial role in assessing each component of AI systems.

Data Quality Metrics

Data quality significantly influences the predictability of outcomes. To gauge the quality of data, we need to define appropriate metrics aligned with the evaluation of AI-integrated applications. The metrics are determined according to the modality of the provided data. We will explore some of these metrics.

Completeness

Metric Definition: Ensures all required data elements are present in the desired format.

Example: In an e-commerce application, customer details such as name, address, and email should comply with the application's format.

Quality Evaluation: Measure the presence of necessary data fields for each record. Identify missing or incomplete data.

Uniqueness

Metric Definition: Ensures no duplicate data points exist.

Example: In e-commerce applications, customer details should have no duplicated entries. The combination of mandatory data fields needed to identify a customer should be unique.

Quality Evaluation: Check for duplicate records based on unique identifiers. Ensure no two records share identical key information.

Consistency

Metric Definition: Ensures all data elements for a given feature adhere to the same representation.
Example: Customer's order details in an e-commerce application should consistently follow the same format.
Quality Evaluation: Check for consistency in data formats, units, and representations across the dataset. For example, ensure that date values consistently follow a specific format.

Accuracy

Metric Definition: Defines the ability to identify a data point without ambiguity based on its characteristics or description.
Example: In an e-commerce application, past transactions should be accurately displayed in the order history.
Quality Evaluation: Validate data against trusted sources. Compare data points with external references to ensure accuracy.

Timeliness

Metric Definition: Indicates the relevance of data at the time it is used.
Example: In an e-commerce application, cancelled orders may not be valuable when analyzing on-time delivery metrics for a seller.
Quality Evaluation: Assess whether the data is current and relevant for the intended use. Time-sensitive data should be up to date.

Validity

Metric Definition: Indicates the validity of the data in its current context.
Example: In an e-commerce application, past deals provided by the application are no longer valid after the offer period ends.
Quality Evaluation: Check if the data is valid and applicable for the current business rules and requirements. Ensure that outdated or expired information is not used.

By accessing data against these metrics, organizations can evaluate their data's overall quality and make informed decisions based on reliable and accurate information.

Now, let's examine these metrics at a more granular level, considering different data modalities. We'll discuss data quality metrics for structured data, unstructured text, audio, and images.

Structured Data Metrics

- Data Label Noise: Analyzes labels in training data to detect inconsistencies.

- Data Homogeneity: Analyzes data to find format inconsistencies, such as date formats, punctuation, address patterns, etc.

- Class Overlap: Analyzes data points that could potentially overlap across classes.

- Class Imbalance: Analyzes data to find class imbalance by looking at other properties of data beyond counting the number of points per class.

Unstructured Text Metrics

- Data Coherence: Identifies data that are like each other or lack a standard format.

- Label Consistency: Identifies data labelled inconsistently due to different standards followed by team members handling the data.

- Data Balance: Identifies the distribution of data across categories of data. It identifies under-represented or over-represented data categories.

- Outlier Detection: Identifies outliers in the given data by representing the data in a semantic space.

Audio Metrics

- Signal-to-Noise Ratio (SNR): Measures the ratio of the audio signal's strength to background noise. Higher SNR indicates better audio quality.

- Clarity: Assesses the overall clarity and intelligibility of the audio.

- Distortion: Measures any unwanted changes or disruptions in the audio signal. Minimal distortion is preferred for accurate representation of the original sound.

Image Metrics

- Resolution: The number of pixels in an image, usually expressed as width x height (e.g., 1920x1080). Higher resolution generally results in clearer and more detailed images.

- Sharpness: The clarity of edges and fine details in the image.

- Color Accuracy: Measures how accurately the colors in the image represent the true colors of the scene.

- Contrast: The difference in brightness between the darkest and lightest parts of the image.

- Brightness: The overall luminance or intensity of the image.

- Noise: Unwanted variations in brightness or color in areas of uniform appearance.

- Distortion: Any aberrations or deformations in the image compared to the original scene. Minimizing distortion ensures a faithful representation of the subject.

Measuring data quality instils confidence in the predictability of AI systems. Higher quality data indicates the ability to apply transformation techniques to achieve high accuracy.

AI-based Quality Metrics

Quality engineering metrics are well-established in the industry. This section will focus on understanding quality metrics unique to evaluating AI-integrated applications.

In a previous chapter, we discussed the statistical evaluation technique for assessing probabilistic systems. The metrics used in this technique help evaluate the quality of AI-based applications. Using the same techniques, we will discuss key metrics that should be evaluated to measure the quality of these applications.

Metrics derived from the Confusion Matrix provide valuable insights into the quality of AI-based applications. Revisiting the nomenclature of the Confusion Matrix will highlight the metrics to be evaluated.

Key metrics for evaluating AI-based applications include:

Accuracy

Definition: The ratio of correctly predicted instances to the total instances.

Formula: (TP + TN) / (TP + TN + FP + FN)

Interpretation: Accuracy is a commonly used measure of the model's correctness across all classes. However, it may not be suitable for datasets with varying data distribution across the classes, as the output may be biased towards over-represented classes.

Precision

Definition: The ratio of correctly predicted positive observations to the total predicted positives.

Formula: TP / (TP + FP)

Interpretation: Precision focuses on the accuracy of positive predictions. It is particularly useful when the impact of false positives is high. High Precision values indicate fewer false positives.

Recall (Sensitivity or True Positive Rate)

Definition: The ratio of correctly predicted positive observations to all observations in the actual class.
Formula: TP / (TP + FN)
Interpretation: Recall measures the model's ability to capture all relevant instances of the positive class. When the impact of false negatives is high on the end results, this metric is used. A high recall means the model is good at identifying most positive instances.

Usage in Evaluation

Balancing Accuracy, Precision, and Recall

- Although accuracy is a common metric, it might not be sufficient, especially in imbalanced datasets. For example, in a binary classification problem where 95% of instances belong to class A and 5% belong to class B, a model predicting all instances as class A would achieve 95% accuracy but might not be useful.

- Precision and recall provide a more nuanced view. Precision helps to understand false positives, and recall helps to understand false negatives.

- Depending on the specific goals and constraints of the problem, you might need to balance precision and recall. This can be achieved using metrics like the F1 score, which is the harmonic mean of precision and recall.

Threshold Adjustment

- In many classification problems, you can adjust the decision threshold of the model to trade-off between precision and recall. A lower threshold might increase recall but decrease precision, and vice versa.

- The Receiver Operating Characteristic (ROC) curve and Precision-Recall (PR) curve are useful tools to visualize the trade-offs between sensitivity and specificity, or precision and recall, at different thresholds.

Domain-Specific Considerations

- The choice between precision and recall depends on the specific application. In some cases, false positives might be more acceptable than false negatives, or vice versa.

- For example, in a medical diagnosis scenario, high recall might be more important to ensure that all cases of a disease are captured, even at the cost of more false positives.

In summary, accuracy, precision, and recall are essential metrics to evaluate the effectiveness of a machine learning model. Choosing the most appropriate metric depends on the nature of the problem, the characteristics of the dataset, and the specific goals and constraints of the application.

As a Quality Engineer specializing in testing AI-based solutions, the foundation for ensuring the reliability of these systems lies in defining and evaluating key quality metrics. These metrics range from data quality metrics, such as completeness, uniqueness, consistency, accuracy, timeliness, and validity, to AI-based quality metrics, such as precision, recall, and accuracy. Understanding the nuances of these metrics, their trade-offs, and domain-specific considerations is essential for Quality Engineers working with AI-infused applications.

Incorporating AI specific testing techniques

We have understood the various components of AI applications. We have also discussed the metrics needed to evaluate the quality of these applications. In this section, we will delve deep into testing AI infused applications.

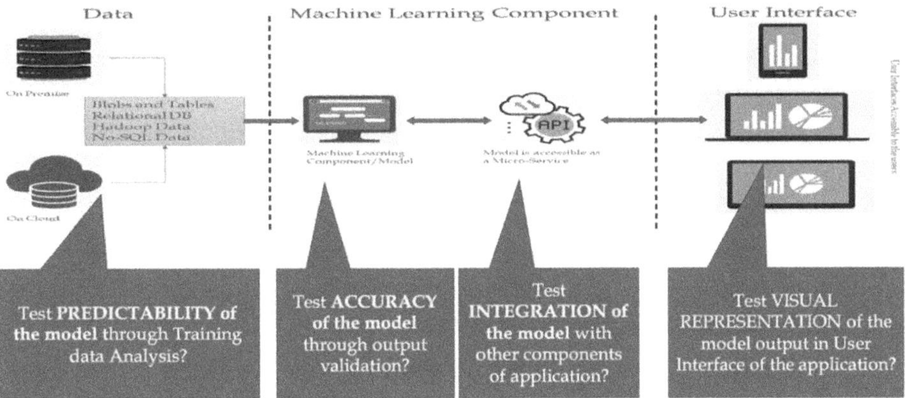

Figure 5.2: Error! No text of specified style in document. 2 Key objectives in testing AI Infused application

We have discussed the need to validate the quality of Data, integration layer and user interface represented in Figure 5-1. We will discuss the unique aspects of testing AI infused application components.

Data Quality Assessment

As per Mckinsley & company, Missing or incomplete data, i.e there's information available for all parameters in some cases while missing for certain parameters in other cases in the same data set. These inconsistencies result in skewed or faulty learning, which ultimately leads to failed solutions.
The quality of data available to train machine learning models and cross validation data set plays a significant role in ensuring the machine learning model/component meets the defined expectations.
The answers to the following questions from chapter 3 is still unanswered:

- Do all the business combinations sufficiently represented in training data?

- Does your data consist of bias towards certain data combinations?

- How will you test when the training data is not available for validation?

- How will you replicate training data bias in test data?

To answer the questions above, evaluating the quality of data from a data science perspective is necessary to improve the predictability of each of the machine learning component available in the application. These evaluation techniques can achieve this.

- Quality of data analysis to ensure the completeness of training data. Using a metrics-based approach the data quality can be evaluated. The data metrics defined in the previous section should be computed and evaluated.

- Data split analysis will provide insights into the bias available in the training/test data and how it should be handled in the machine learning model. This approach will provide the capability to identify the under-represented or over-represented data combinations. When the data bias is identified one of the following decisions needs to be taken.

- Based on the business functionality the decision to retain the data to simulate real time data combination.

- If the data combination representation does not reflect real time data, then data normalization approach should be considered. Synthetic data generation or provisioning of additional data points for under-represented data combinations should be considered.

- Evaluation of sufficiency of training and test data can be achieved through combinatorial testing method to provide insights into representation of every business combination.

Data testing method for AI infused application should provide capabilities on following validations:

- Evaluate the sensitivity of the input data towards the predicted output. Features that are hyper-sensitive towards the machine learning models using Neural Networks or Support Vector machine.

- Centrality of data distribution in each cluster can be evaluated and ensured using data split analysis. Aligning the data to meet normal distribution is preferred.

- Sparseness of data in clusters/splits that are underrepresented can also be evaluated. This will ensure data can be supplemented to improve the representation of these combinations.

Test Design

Before we explore the test design approach for AI Infused Application (AIIA) testing, let's explore the concept of Combinatorial Test Design (CTD)

Combinatorial Test Design

Combinatorial Test Design (CTD) is a method of testing that involves identifying the possible combinations of input parameters and their values, and then selecting a subset of these combinations to test. The goal of CTD is to cover all possible interactions between the input parameters and to identify defects that may arise from these interactions. CTD is particularly useful when testing complex systems with multiple input parameters, as it helps to reduce the number of test cases while still providing thorough coverage.

Let's consider an example of a payment system that requires a secure and user-friendly payment process. The system supports four payment methods: Credit card, Debit card, Internet Banking, and UPI. The user interface should display a list of available payment methods, and upon selection, the user should be directed to a secure payment gateway. The payment gateway should display fields for the user to enter their payment details, which vary depending on the payment method. The system should validate the user's payment details and authenticate the transaction, and then process the payment upon successful authentication.

Key Elements of CTD

Points of Variations (Attributes and Values): These are the input parameters that can vary and affect the behavior of the system. In our example, the points of variations are:

- Payment Method (Credit card, Debit card, Internet Banking, UPI)
- Payment Details (Card number, Expiry date, CVV number, OTP for Credit and Debit card; UPI ID, password, OTP for UPI; Bank ID, password, OTP for Internet Banking)
- Authentication (Successful, Unsuccessful)
- Payment Processing (Successful, Unsuccessful)
- Confirmation Message (Displayed, Not Displayed).

Business Rules: These are the constraints that define the behavior of the system. In our example, the business rules are:

- The system should validate the user's payment details and authenticate the transaction.
- The system should process the payment transaction upon successful authentication.
- The system should display a confirmation message upon successful payment.
- The payment processing time should be less than 2 seconds.

Test Scenarios: These are the specific combinations of input parameters and values that are selected for testing. In our example, the test scenarios are generated using the level 3 interaction, which means that we combine three points of variation at a time. Some of few resulting test scenarios are:

- Credit card, Card number, Expiry date, CVV number, OTP, Successful, Successful, Displayed
- Credit card, Card number, Expiry date, CVV number, OTP, Unsuccessful, Unsuccessful, Not Displayed
- Debit card, Card number, Expiry date, CVV number, OTP, Successful, Successful, Displayed
- Internet Banking, Bank ID, password, OTP, Successful, Successful, Displayed.

We can see that the test scenarios are generated by combining the points of variation in a systematic way. For example, the first test scenario combines the payment method "Credit card" with the payment details "Card number, Expiry date, CVV number, OTP" and the authentication and payment processing outcomes "Successful" and "Displayed". This test scenario covers a specific combination of input parameters and values that may interact with each other in a particular way.

By generating test scenarios in this way, we can ensure that we cover all possible interactions between the input parameters and identify defects that may arise from these interactions. The business rules are used to eliminate test scenarios that are not valid or relevant, and to ensure that the test scenarios are consistent with the expected behavior of the system.

The advantages of using Combinatorial Test Design (CTD) in terms of test coverage, optimization of test cases, and ease of maintaining test scenarios in a model-based testing approach:

- Improved Test Coverage: CTD ensures that all possible combinations of input parameters are covered, which leads to more comprehensive testing and increased test coverage. By identifying all possible interactions between input parameters, CTD helps to detect defects that may arise from these interactions.

- Optimization of Test Cases: CTD reduces the number of test cases required to cover all possible combinations of input parameters. By selecting a subset of test scenarios that cover all possible interactions, CTD optimizes the test cases and reduces the testing effort.

- Ease of Maintaining Test Scenarios: In a model-based testing approach, CTD makes it easier to maintain test scenarios. When changes are made to the system, the model can be updated, and new test scenarios can be generated automatically. This ensures that the test scenarios remain relevant and up-to-date.

- Reduced Test Data: CTD reduces the amount of test data required, as it focuses on the most critical combinations of input parameters. This reduces the testing effort and makes it easier to manage test data.

- Improved Test Efficiency: CTD improves test efficiency by reducing the number of test cases and the amount of test data required. This leads to faster testing and reduced testing costs.

- Early Defect Detection: CTD helps to detect defects early in the testing cycle, which reduces the overall cost of defect fixing and improves the quality of the system.

- Model-Based Testing: CTD is particularly useful in model-based testing, where the system is modeled using a formal specification language. The model can be used to generate test scenarios automatically, which ensures that the test scenarios are consistent with the expected behavior of the system.

- Reusability: CTD enables reusability of test scenarios across different testing cycles and environments. This reduces the testing effort and makes it easier to maintain test scenarios.

- Improved Collaboration: CTD improves collaboration between testers, developers, and other stakeholders, as it provides a common understanding of the system's behavior and the test scenarios.

- Scalability: CTD is scalable and can be applied to systems of varying complexity, making it a versatile testing approach.

By using Combinatorial Test Design, testers can ensure that their testing is comprehensive, efficient, and effective, and that they are detecting defects early in the testing cycle. In summary, Combinatorial Test Design is a method of testing that involves identifying the possible combinations of input parameters and their values, and then selecting a subset of these combinations to test. By applying CTD to our example payment system, we can generate a set of test scenarios that cover all possible interactions between the input parameters and identify defects that may arise from these interactions.

Now that we have understood the concept of CTD, let's explore Test design approach AI infused application testing given below:

- The functional specifications are one of the key inputs to identify all the test cases. All the various points of variation in the application should be identified. This input will be used to create the test scenario to be tested.

- Unlike traditional deterministic applications, data plays a significant role in the development of AI infused applications. The data insights are an important input to create a comprehensive test design. The key insights needed for the same are:

o Properties of data identified through profiling of data. Profiling of data provides insights of lexical diversity. These variations should be provided in the test cases to ensure comprehensive coverage. For example, in a virtual assistant, the text data used to train the application should have variations like abbreviations, variations of active and passive sentences, language accents, sentence complexity etc.

o Representation of data combinations in data are key input to determining the data bias. Using techniques like data bucket analysis, the data combinations are categorized based on the number of data points available for each data combination.

The average number of data points per data combination is considered as normal representation. The data combinations with significantly less data points are considered as under-represented data combination. Likewise, data combinations with significantly more data points are considered as over-represented data combinations.

For example, in an ecommerce application, when average number of orders per day of men's t-shirts for different sizes is 100. If number of orders of t-shirts for Large size is 15 and for eXtra Small size is 200 then data combination for Large size is considered as under-represented and that of eXtra Small size is over-represented.

The data representation should be in line with real-time data patterns. If data sample selected does not reflect this pattern, then data should either be provisioned, or synthetic data should be generated to reflect the same.

- The combination of functionality and data insights should be considered to create the test combinations to test. Using model-based testing approach, the test combinations can be generated. One such solution is given below.

Combinatorial Test Design (CTD) approach is used to identify the points of variation in the test set and uses the same to generate the various test scenario with 100% test coverage. The key to identifying the points of variations for creating the CTD model is to know the features selected for the ML model creation. These features could be direct or derived. A tester needs to know the final set of direct or derived features selected for the model to identify the points of variations. Examples of how structured data can be used as points of variation for Combinatorial Test Design is given below. Let's take a Regression problem, where we are trying to predict the number of defects that will be raised on each week of the testing phase of a project. We have identified the points of variation based on the features selected for creating this model. A representative CTD model is given in the figure below.

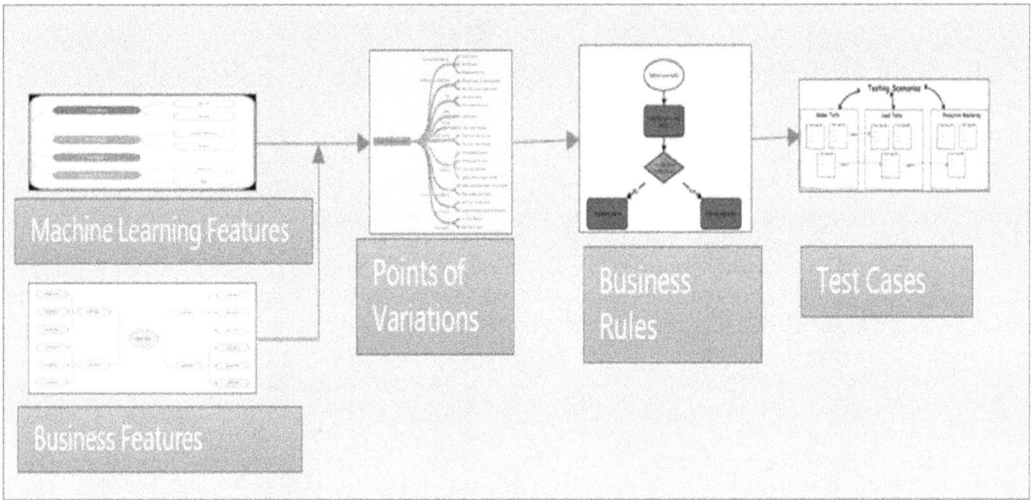

Figure 5.3: *An example of combining business functionality and machine learning data insights*

This model will provide a list of test combinations when we use pair-wise testing approach. Increasing the coverage requirement will provide more test combinations.

Test Data

The test case readiness implies us to move to next step i.e. test data provisioning. Some of the key considerations in provisioning data for testing AI infused Applications are:

- Data provisioned should reflect the real-time pattern in representation of data for each of the data combinations. As discussed in the e-commerce application example, the t-shirt size data should represent the real-time sales pattern. When some data combinations selected in the test data is under-represented, additional data points should be provisioned.

- Data provisioned should have variation in data points to evaluate the consistent behaviour of the AI systems. In the e-commerce application's order management system, order data should be available for all sizes of t-shirts and colours provided by the seller. If a certain t-shirt size and colour combination is never purchased, then the data should reflect zero orders.

- Test data should also adhere to data quality metrics standards explained in previous chapters.

There is a possibility of unavailability of sufficient data points in the system to reflect certain data combinations. Then data should be generated synthetically in these scenarios. The capability to generate data synthetically can be achieved through the following approaches:

- Manually generate data to match the data patterns needed for testing. This approach can be achieved by the Quality Engineering team. An alternate approach to generate data is through crowd sourcing. A crowd source approach can be used to generate voice-based data inputs to test virtual assistants enable with voice input.

- Automated synthetic data generation capability has been available for structured data for quite some time now. There are many Open Source and COTS tools available. Tools like GenRocket, Query Surge are COTS tools while Data Factory, SQL Data Generator are some of the open source tools available for structured data generation.

- Generating synthetic data for unstructured data needs AI or machine learning capabilities.

o For generating synthetic unstructured text input, linguistic ML models are used. These models are capable of transforming reference data to generate new sentences. Markov Chain Text Generation and Recurrent Neural Networks (RNN) are some of the well know methods to generate text data.

o Images can also be generated synthetically using advanced AI techniques like Generative Adversarial Networks (GAN) and Variation Autoencoder (VAE).

o Audio data can also be synthetically generated using AI techniques like RNN and WaveGANs. Using Text to Speech conversion is another approach used to generate synthetic audio data.

Provisioning or synthetically generating test data will provide sufficient data points to evaluate the outcome of the application.

Testing Artificial Intelligence/ Machine Learning Component

Considering AI or ML components are the core of AI infused systems, quality of these components is critical to evaluating the quality of these applications/systems. In the previous section we discussed metrics to evaluate the quality of these components. Let's discuss the approach to testing components in isolation.

Traditionally, the AI or ML components were tested using a unit testing approach. However, with ensemble of AI/ML models being used, this approach cannot be considered for functional testing. We have discussed these challenges in previous chapters.

The following approach should be followed to evaluate the quality of AI components

- **Evaluating probabilistic nature of AI components**: AI or machine leaning components are the contributors to probabilistic nature of AI application. As discussed in chapter 2, testing these applications needs a specialized approach. The approach is discussed below:

Considering these applications cannot have an absolute pass or fail results for test cases, we need to adopt an approach to evaluate the probability of the result.

This approach is illustrated in the context of a classification solution of predicting the root cause analysis of a production ticket. The root cause prediction solution will use historic data to understand the correlation of ticket details and the root cause.

When a new ticket is raised, the root cause prediction AI model will provide the predicted root causes and their associated probability score. It would represent Environment error with 45% confidence, Data error with 20% confidence etc. adding up to 100% confidence score. Based on this output the root cause with highest confidence score i.e. environment error is presented as the output.

In the above scenario, though environment error is presented as the top result, however the statistical confidence score from the model was less than 50%. Should you accept this output? What would be an alternate approach?

Let's take another approach to validate the outcome. We will set a threshold confidence score of 75%, meaning that if the output of our prediction model has a confidence score above 75%, we will accept it as is. However, if the confidence score is below 75%, we will further evaluate the output using statistical methods with multiple data points to ensure accuracy and reliability. Additionally, if the output of the prediction model indicates an "Environment error" with a confidence score greater than 75%, we will compare the output with the expected result, and this comparison will determine whether the test case passes or fails, providing a clear outcome for the testing process.

Summarizing, the output of the AI model will be accepted as is, only if the confidence score of the output is higher than the threshold confidence score.

- **Testing of AI components needs statistical evaluation**: In the example of ticket root cause prediction, the confidence score of Environment error was less than the Threshold confidence score. In these situations, we need to perform statistical evaluation of the output by executing the same test case with different variations of data points.

The execution result is consolidated and the statistical evaluation metrics discussed earlier will be used to determine if the test case has passed or failed. The metrics: accuracy, precision and recall should be used to evaluate the outcome of the test results.

- Testing with large Datasets testing with APIs: Evaluating the outcome of the test cases statistically requires sufficiently large number of data points. Considering these test cases are being executed post unit testing in system integration test or functional test phase, end to end testing will not be cost effective.

- These test cases should be executed at API layer to ensure testing can be accomplished quickly and cost effectively.

- Consistency of the result is another key aspect of evaluating AI or Machine learning based components. Given the input data is the same to these components, the predicted output should always be the same. If there is inconsistency in the predicted output, then the AI or ML component is considered sensitive or inconsistent.

Test End-to-End Application

In the previous section, we discussed how the AI or ML components are evaluated. The need to perform an end-to-end testing of the application will ensure a holistic testing approach. The following best practices should be followed to accomplish the same:

- **The User Interface of the application should be tested to evaluate the adherence to requirements specification. We discussed the testing of User Interface in detail earlier in the chapter.**

- **AI or ML components should be considered as a black-box and the output of the results should be evaluated to ensure the expected test result is obtained.**

- **End-to-End testing is time consuming and cost ineffective when**

executed for large test dataset, hence should be performed as a regression test.

- **End-to-end testing should be automated as much as possible and should be executed in unattended mode as part of DevOps pipeline.**

In conclusion, testing AI-infused applications is a complex but crucial process that involves evaluating various components to ensure the quality and reliability of the system. The focus on data quality assessment is paramount, as the success of machine learning models heavily depends on the quality and representativeness of the training data. Addressing questions related to data completeness, biases, and sufficiency is essential to enhance the predictability of AI components.

Test design for AI-infused applications requires a comprehensive approach, considering functional specifications and the unique role of data in the development process. Combinatorial Test Design (CTD) emerges as a valuable technique, utilizing mathematical models to identify points of variation and generate test scenarios with maximum coverage.

Ensuring regulatory compliance in AI-driven solutions

The approach to testing AI infused applications was discussed in the previous section. There are critical and mandatory regulatory compliances that AI-driven solutions must adhere to. Some of these regulatory compliances are discussed in this section.

Sensitivity Detection and Adversarial Robustness

We discussed the need for consistent behavior of the AI components. The need to take this evaluation to sensitivity is critical towards performance evaluation of AI based solutions. In simple terms, Sensitivity is the measure of vulnerability of AI system to modify the output to minor or trivial changes to input data. Adversarial robustness is the ability of a machine learning model to resist adversarial attacks that involve making small, carefully crafted modifications to input data to deceive the model.

To evaluate the sensitivity detection and adversarial robustness of an AI solutions, the input data is modified to generate data with minor variation.

Text Data can be modified using some of the commonly used perturbation techniques like introducing noise, replacement of synonyms, paraphrasing of sentences etc.

Similarly, for image data the perturbation techniques could be like Contrast, brightness, colour change, rotating images, zooming images etc.

Audio data can also be modified using techniques like introducing noise like white noise, background noise etc.

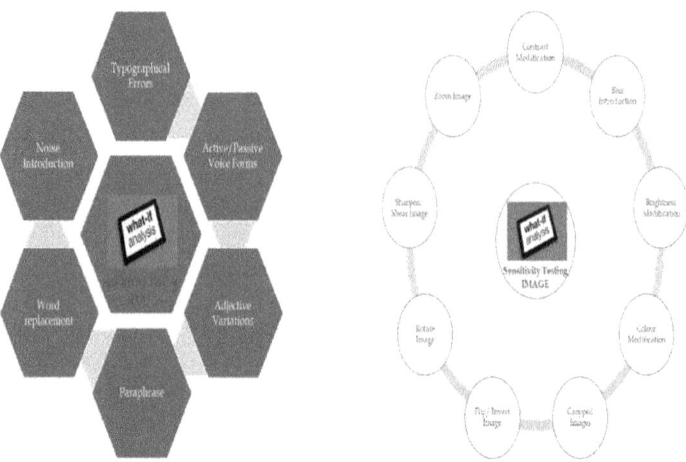

Figure 5.4: *Perturbations to Text and Image data for Sensitivity Assessment*

Legal and Ethical Behavior

Legal and ethical compliance for AI systems is a critical consideration to ensure responsible development, deployment, and use of artificial intelligence. The specific requirements may vary by jurisdiction, but there are several common principles and guidelines that are recognized internationally. Here are some key legal and ethical considerations for AI systems:

Legal Compliance

- Data Protection and Privacy Laws: Compliance with data protection and privacy regulations, such as the General Data Protection Regulation (GDPR) in the European Union is business critical mandate. This includes obtaining informed consent, ensuring data minimization and providing individuals with the right to access and control their data.

- Anti-discrimination Laws: AI systems must adhere to anti-discrimination laws to prevent bias and unfair treatment. In the United States, for example, the Civil Rights Act prohibits discrimination based on race, color, religion, sex, or national origin.

- Intellectual Property Laws: Respect intellectual property laws and ensure that the development and use of AI systems do not infringe on patents, copyrights or trademarks.

- Contractual Obligations: AI developers and users should comply with contractual agreements governing the development, licensing and use of

AI technologies.

- Liability and Accountability: Define clear lines of liability and accountability in case of harm caused by AI systems. This may involve determining responsibility between developers, users and other stakeholders.

- Cybersecurity Laws: Adhere to cybersecurity laws and standards to protect AI systems from unauthorized access, data breaches and other security threats.

Ethical Compliance

- Fairness and Bias Mitigation: Ensure fairness in AI systems by addressing biases and mitigating discrimination. AI algorithms should be designed and tested to avoid favoring or disadvantaging particular groups.

- Transparency: Strive for transparency in AI decision-making processes. Make efforts to explain how the AI system works and provide clear explanations for its decisions when possible.

- Accountability and Responsibility: Establish accountability mechanisms and ethical guidelines for the development, deployment, and use of AI systems. This includes responsible use of AI technologies and a commitment to addressing negative impacts.

- Human Oversight: Maintain human oversight and intervention where necessary, especially in critical decision-making processes, to ensure ethical considerations are considered.

- Informed Consent: Obtain informed consent from individuals whose data is used by AI systems, especially in cases where the data is sensitive, or the impact of AI decisions is significant.

- Environmental Impact: Consider the environmental impact of AI systems, particularly energy consumption, and strive to minimize negative effects on the environment.

- International Standards and Guidelines: Adhere to international standards and guidelines, such as those provided by organizations like the IEEE, the Partnership on AI, and other industry-specific bodies.

- Public and Stakeholder Engagement: Engage with the public and relevant stakeholders to incorporate diverse perspectives and ensure that the deployment of AI systems aligns with societal values.

Maintaining regulatory compliance in AI-powered solutions demands a holistic approach that tackles both technical and ethical aspects. Evaluating the sensitivity detection and adversarial resilience of AI systems is crucial, which involves altering input data to determine vulnerabilities. Furthermore, legal and ethical factors play a significant role in the responsible creation, implementation and utilization of AI. Compliance with data protection regulations, anti-discrimination rules, intellectual property laws, contractual obligations, liability and accountability frameworks, and cybersecurity regulations is imperative. Ethical compliance encompasses addressing biases, promoting transparency, instituting accountability measures, incorporating human supervision, obtaining informed consent, considering environmental impacts, adhering to international norms, and engaging with relevant stakeholders. By following these guidelines, organizations can foster trust, protect individual rights, and contribute to the responsible development of artificial intelligence.

Staying up to date with the ever-evolving AI ethics and regulatory landscape is crucial, as it ensures alignment with societal values in a constantly changing legal and ethical environment. By embracing this comprehensive approach, organizations can effectively navigate the complexities of regulatory compliance in AI-driven solutions and ensure their technology aligns with both technical and ethical standards.

Conclusion

A comprehensive approach is vital when navigating the complexities of Quality Engineering for AI-integrated applications. The journey starts by examining AI-focused quality metrics and objectives, highlighting the importance of data quality. Metrics such as completeness, uniqueness, consistency, accuracy, timeliness, and validity act as guiding principles, ensuring a strong and reliable data foundation tailored to AI applications' unique requirements. The focus then narrows to various data modalities, revealing specific metrics for structured data, unstructured text, audio, and images. From analyzing label noise in structured data to assessing coherence in unstructured text, these custom metrics demonstrate the nuanced understanding needed to evaluate the quality of information used in AI systems. The narrative smoothly transitions to AI-centric quality metrics, exploring the subtleties of accuracy, precision, and recall. These metrics serve as key indicators for assessing probabilistic systems, providing insights into their correctness, false positives, and false negatives. Balancing these metrics is crucial, leading to the use of the F1 score and threshold adjustments to navigate the challenges of imbalanced datasets and particular application objectives. With a solid foundation in data and AI quality metrics, the investigation delves into AI-specific testing techniques. The emphasis on data quality assessment becomes paramount, examining the completeness of training data, addressing biases, and ensuring data sufficiency. Combinatorial Test Design (CTD) stands out as a powerful technique, using mathematical models to identify variation points and generate test scenarios with exceptional coverage. As the journey progresses, the focus shifts to the vital area of regulatory compliance. Sensitivity detection and adversarial robustness become essential, underlining the need to evaluate AI systems' vulnerability and resistance to intentional input alterations. Legal and ethical considerations form a network of responsibilities, covering data protection, anti-discrimination laws, intellectual property, accountability frameworks, and cybersecurity. Pursuing fairness, transparency, and environmental responsibility becomes integral to the ethical development of AI.

In conclusion, incorporating AI into applications requires a meticulous approach. The narrative spans from scrutinizing data quality metrics to evaluating AI-based quality metrics, and from AI-specific testing techniques to the necessity of regulatory compliance. The convergence of technical excellence, ethical considerations, and legal compliance serves as a guiding compass for Quality Engineers traversing the intricate landscape of AI-integrated applications. The journey emphasizes the need for robust algorithms and the responsibility to ensure ethical implementation, legal compliance, and unwavering quality in the age of artificial intelligence.

Exercise: Test Your Understanding

Answer the following questions and test your understanding of learning from Chapter 5:

Q. 1. What is the primary purpose of the "Completeness" metric in data quality assessment for AI-infused applications?

- A. To measure the ratio of correctly predicted instances to total instances
- B. To ensure that all mandatory data elements are available in the desired format
- C. To evaluate the sensitivity of input data towards the predicted output
- D. To assess the relevance of data at the time it is used

Q. 2. Which testing technique utilizes a mathematical model to identify points of variation and generate test scenarios for maximum coverage in AI-infused applications?

- A. Unit Testing
- B. Random Testing
- C. Combinatorial Test Design (CTD)
- D. Black Box Testing

Q. 3. What is the key consideration for evaluating the quality of AI components, considering their probabilistic nature?

- A. Absolute pass or fail results for test cases
- B. Human intervention in decision-making processes
- C. Statistical evaluation of the output based on confidence scores
- D. Adherence to contractual agreements

Q. 4. Which aspect is critical for assessing the vulnerability of AI systems to minor changes in input data and resisting adversarial attacks?

- A. Sensitivity Detection and Adversarial Robustness
- B. Precision and Recall Metrics
- C. Data Quality Metrics
- D. Completeness in Data Representation

Q. 5. What is a key legal compliance consideration for AI systems according to the content?

A. Consistency of AI component results

B. Adherence to international standards and guidelines

C. Evaluating the sensitivity of input data

D. Providing clear explanations for AI decisions

Chapter 6

Leveraging AI to Enhance QE Practices

In the previous chapter, we discussed the various components of AI systems and the method to evaluate the quality of each component.

This chapter will focus on another aspect of AI and Quality Engineering. We will discuss the importance of using Artificial Intelligence in improving the efficiency of Quality Engineering practices. Use cases like test case generation, synthetic test data generation and defect management are some of the few focus areas. In addition to the above, the QE tools and frameworks infused with AI capabilities will be explored in detail. Adopt AI in Quality engineering comes with its own challenges, and we will delve into these challenges and the approach to overcome them.

In this chapter, we will discuss the following topics:

- Devels into the applications of AI in quality engineering to optimize activities.

- Discover how AI can be used for test case generation, test data generation, and defect prediction to enhance the testing process.

- Learn how to seamlessly integrate AI-based tools and frameworks into the quality engineering process for improved efficiency.

- Explore the benefits and challenges of adopting AI in quality engineering, and how it can revolutionize the way we approach quality assurance

AI-powered quality engineering

Artificial intelligence capabilities can be adopted in quality engineering based on the type of solution it supports. These solution types can be broadly categorized based on the capability they support. We are enforcing these basics building blocks of AI infusion in Quality Engineering through Quality Platform.

- **Augment** is the ability to enhance the existing capability by boosting the output. In the realm of quality engineering, AI applications play a pivotal role in augmenting human capabilities, thereby enhancing the effectiveness and efficiency of quality assurance processes. By leveraging AI-powered tools and technologies, Quality Engineers can augment their skills and expertise to achieve better outcomes in various aspects of quality engineering.

For instance, AI-driven test automation frameworks empower QE teams to automate repetitive and time-consuming testing tasks, such as test case generation, test script creation, synthetically generating test cases and test execution. These frameworks harness machine learning algorithms to intelligently identify patterns in application behavior, thereby enabling the generation of robust test cases that cover a wide range of scenarios.

Furthermore, AI-based virtual assistants and chatbots can augment the capabilities of Quality engineers by providing real-time assistance and guidance throughout the testing process. These virtual assistants can answer queries, provide recommendations, and offer insights based on historical data and best practices, thereby enabling quality engineers to make informed decisions and streamline their workflows.

In essence, the augmentation of quality engineering using AI enables QE teams to leverage advanced technologies to overcome challenges, enhance productivity, efficiency and effectiveness in software development, which directly influences quality.

- **Analysis and Advise**: Analyzing data and deriving insights to optimize processes is a critical aspect of quality engineering, and defect management serves as a prime example of utilizing AI-driven use cases. AI applications play a pivotal role in facilitating comprehensive analysis of software quality metrics and performance indicators, empowering QE teams to delve deeper into their products and processes. Through AI-powered analytics tools and techniques, Quality engineers can sift through vast amounts of testing data to uncover trends, patterns and anomalies that may impact software quality.

For instance, AI-driven anomaly detection algorithms can scrutinize historical test data and performance metrics to flag deviations from expected behavior, such as spikes in error rates or fluctuations in application performance. By identifying such anomalies proactively, QE teams can implement corrective measures to mitigate risks and uphold the reliability of their software systems. Similarly, AI-powered predictive analytics tools enable QE teams to forecast potential quality issues and performance bottlenecks ahead of time, allowing them to take preventive actions to optimize software quality and performance.

In essence, leveraging AI applications for analysis and advising in quality engineering empowers QE teams to make data-driven decisions and continuously enhance their software products' quality. Through actionable insights provided by AI, QE professionals can effectively optimize processes, improve efficiency and deliver high-quality software solutions to end-users.

- **Automate** provides the ability to reduce manual effort by performing repeatable tasks using AI capability.

Automation is a cornerstone of quality engineering and AI applications play a pivotal role in driving automation across various aspects of the QE lifecycle. Using AI-powered automation tools and frameworks, QE teams can streamline their testing processes, reduce manual effort and accelerate the delivery of high-quality software products.

One of the key areas where AI-driven automation is transforming quality engineering is in test case generation and test script creation. Traditional methods of test case design often rely on manual effort and domain expertise, which can be time-consuming and error prone. AI-based test case generation tools leverage machine learning algorithms to analyze application requirements, codebase and user behavior data to automatically generate test cases that cover a wide range of scenarios and edge cases.

Furthermore, AI-powered test automation frameworks enable intelligent test execution and self-healing capabilities, thereby reducing the need for manual intervention and maintenance. These frameworks leverage machine learning algorithms to adapt to changes in application behavior, automatically update test scripts and identify and resolve test failures in real-time, thereby improving test coverage, reliability and efficiency.

Moreover, AI applications enable automation beyond traditional functional testing to encompass areas such as performance testing, security testing and accessibility testing. By harnessing AI-driven automation tools and techniques, QE teams can extend automation coverage, enhance test accuracy, and ensure overall quality and reliability of their software products.

Here are some of the AI based Quality Platform powered examples:
Example 1: Expected Requirement Analysis capabilities would offer the ability to cognitively assess and prioritize requirements. Ideally, it would automate the evaluation of requirements and integrate it into the modeling workflow. This process should comprehend all requirements and extract keywords using NLP (Open source). This information flow would seamlessly feed into the Test Optimization models.
Example 2: Anticipated Test Case Evaluation capabilities should streamline

existing test cases by grouping them through language analysis methods. The method would aim to eliminate redundancy and inaccuracies in current test cases and test steps, creating an input for the Test Optimization model. The optimization process should effectively handle large quantities of existing tests and align them with a BDD approach to test design. It would be suitable for API, Performance Test, and Big Data solutions and could be increasingly employed for initiating early discussions with clients.

Example 3: Expected Data Quality Assessment capabilities would standardize data quality evaluation using a metric-driven approach. Metrics would be established based on the modality of the input, such as structured data, unstructured text, audio, and images. Additionally, it would offer the capability to implement remediation actions to enhance data quality through suggestions. The Data Quality Assessment should work effectively with structured and unstructured inputs to improve the quality of data utilized in AI-powered applications like classification, clustering, chatbots, and more.

Using AI in Quality Engineering

While delving into the intricacies of AI systems, our focus has been on the imperative need to assess the quality of their components. Let's initiate a comprehensive exploration of evaluating the quality of traditional AI system components: User Interfaces and Integration layers. The forthcoming chapters will explain the evaluation of Data and AI components.

Test Case Generation

AI-powered test case generation involves automatic creation of test cases based on various inputs such as requirements documents, user stories or application code. Traditional methods of test case generation often rely on manual effort and domain expertise, which can be time-consuming and error prone. AI-driven approaches, however, leverage machine learning algorithms to analyze the application under test and automatically generate test cases that cover a wide range of scenarios and edge cases.

These algorithms can analyze the application's behavior, identify critical paths and generate test cases that target specific functionalities, inputs, or user interactions. By harnessing AI for test case generation, QE teams can significantly reduce the time and effort required to design test cases, improve test coverage, and accelerate the testing process.

Example: AI Testing Asset for Test Case Management:

Test Case Management – IVR: The Test Case Management module ensures the creation and maintenance of tests in a GIT repository. An intent repository can be utilized for quick and easy creation and maintenance of tests (when you want to change one intent, you can modify it in the intent repository, and it will be propagated to all tests automatically). Test management supports multiple languages within a single test, meaning – you can create one test flow and run the test in multiple language mutations.

Figure 6.1: *Visualizing test Automation*

Test Data Generation

Test data generation is another critical aspect of software testing, involving the creation of test data sets that simulate real-world scenarios and conditions. AI-powered test data generation tools leverage machine learning algorithms to analyze application requirements, data models, and usage patterns to automatically generate diverse and representative test data sets.

These tools can generate test data that covers a wide range of scenarios, including boundary cases, edge cases, and corner cases, thereby ensuring comprehensive test coverage. Furthermore, AI-driven test data generation tools can optimize test data generation based on factors such as data dependencies, data integrity constraints and performance considerations.

By using AI for test data generation, QE teams can streamline the testing process, reduce reliance on manual data creation, and ensure the quality and diversity of test data sets, leading to more effective and efficient testing outcomes.

Example: AI Testing Asset for Test Case Execution

Test Case Executor - IVR: This tool supports voice bot interaction with voice input or text input types and is capable of testing chatbots. It also supports end-to-end tests for chatbots, or voice bots integrated with web applications (such as agent desktop applications). The tool is easy to use for testing in any environment, be it test or production, and allows for simple language configuration during runtime. Additional features include recording interactions with voice bots, chatbots, or any web app as video or audio records, generating HTML reports, and easy integration with CI/CD tools and test management tools (native JIRA integration). It can also be used as a monitoring tool.

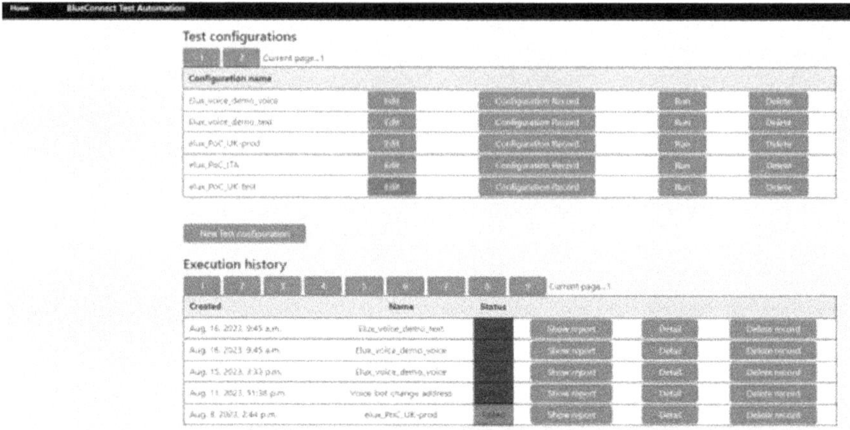

Figure 6.2: Visualizing test results

Defect Prediction

Defect prediction involves the use of AI algorithms to analyze historical data and predict potential defects or quality issues in software applications. These algorithms leverage machine learning techniques to identify patterns, trends, and anomalies in software development and testing data, such as code changes, test results, and defect reports.

By analyzing historical data, AI-driven defect prediction models can identify factors or indicators that are correlated with the occurrence of defects, such as code complexity, developer experience, or testing coverage. These models can then predict the likelihood of defects occurring in specific modules, components or functionalities of the software.

Defect prediction models can help QE teams prioritize testing efforts, allocate resources more effectively, and proactively address potential quality issues before they impact end users. By leveraging AI for defect prediction, organizations can improve the overall quality and reliability of their software products, reduce the cost and effort associated with defect resolution and enhance the customer experience.

Example: AI - Defect Analytics and Prediction

- Defect Analytics and Prediction is a set of cognitive powered tools that provides AI driven defect classification, defect prediction and defect prevention capabilities for a test enterprise.

- Real-time defect root cause and root cause application prediction. (Defect Classification)

- Real-time defect in-flow pattern prediction (Defect Prediction)
- Delivers a prevention roadmap to leads with minimum effort

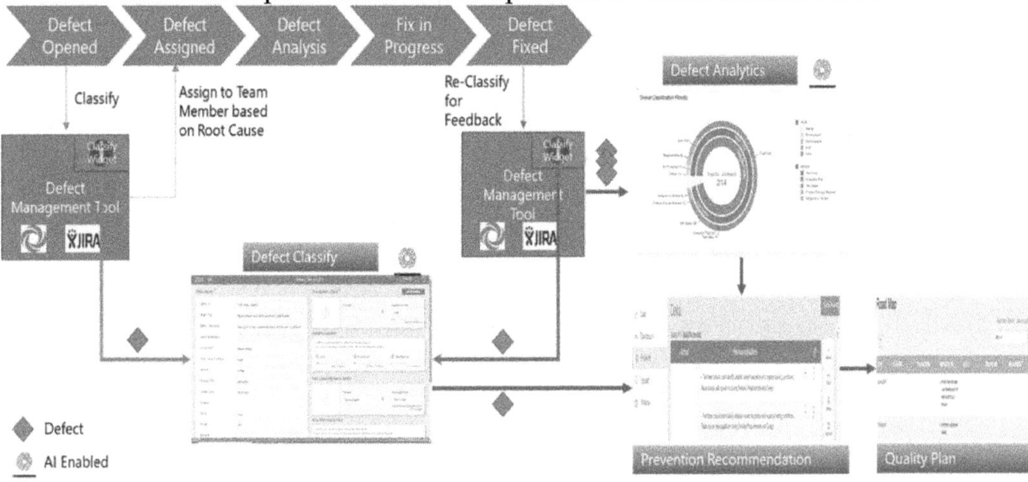

Figure 6.3: A sample AI-enabled Defect Management solution

This model will provide a list of test combinations when we use pair-wise testing approach. Increasing the coverage requirement will provide more test combinations.

Integrating AI-driven tools

In today's rapidly evolving technological landscape, quality engineering stands as a cornerstone for ensuring the reliability, functionality, and performance of software products. Traditional quality engineering processes often rely heavily on manual effort, which can be time-consuming and prone to human error. However, the emergence of artificial intelligence (AI) has paved the way for a new era of automation and intelligence in quality engineering. This exploration delves into the significance, challenges, and best practices of integrating AI-based tools and frameworks into the quality engineering process.

Significance of AI in Quality Engineering

AI plays a pivotal role in modern quality engineering by offering automation, intelligence, and scalability. Through automation, AI-based tools streamline repetitive tasks like test case generation and execution, leading to reduced manual effort and faster testing cycles. Additionally, AI frameworks leverage machine learning algorithms to analyze data, detect patterns, and make informed decisions, thereby enhancing the accuracy and effectiveness of testing processes. Moreover, the scalability of AI-driven solutions allows quality engineering teams to handle large and complex software systems, accommodating the evolving demands of modern software development seamlessly.

Key Components of AI-based Tools and Frameworks

AI-based tools and frameworks encompass essential components such as test automation, test case generation, and predictive analytics. Test automation frameworks powered by AI enable the creation and execution of automated tests, facilitating the identification of test scenarios and prioritization of test cases. Furthermore, AI-driven test case generation tools analyze requirements and design specifications to automatically generate comprehensive test cases, ensuring thorough test coverage and efficiency. Additionally, predictive analytics models analyze historical data to predict potential defects early in the development lifecycle, enabling proactive defect management and risk mitigation.

Challenges in Integration

Integration of AI-based tools and frameworks into quality engineering processes is not without challenges. One major challenge is ensuring data quality and availability, as AI tools require high-quality and representative data for training and analysis. Additionally, the complexity of AI algorithms may hinder their interpretability, raising concerns about transparency and trust. Moreover, integrating AI solutions into existing processes may necessitate organizational changes, training, and collaboration across teams. Furthermore, AI-driven solutions raise ethical and regulatory considerations related to data privacy, bias, and fairness, requiring adherence to ethical guidelines and regulatory requirements.

Best Practices for Integration

To effectively integrate AI-based tools and frameworks into quality engineering processes, organizations should adopt several best practices. Starting small and iterating allows for gradual adoption and assessment of feasibility and effectiveness before scaling up. Foster collaboration and knowledge sharing among quality engineering teams, data scientists, and AI experts to leverage diverse expertise. Invest in data quality and governance initiatives to ensure the availability, accuracy, and relevance of data sets for AI training and analysis. Emphasize transparency and explainability in AI-driven solutions to enhance trust and understanding among stakeholders. Continuously monitor and evaluate the performance of AI-based tools and frameworks to measure success and identify areas for improvement. Here are some of the important tool/frameworks available for AI infusion on Quality Engineering Deliverables:

Tool/Framework	Description	Usability in Quality Engineering	Example(s)
Test Automation Tools	Frameworks for automated testing	Accelerate testing cycles	Selenium, Appium
		Improve test coverage	Robot Framework, Cypress
		Identify and prioritize test cases	TestNG, JUnit
		Adapt to changes in software functionality	PyTest, Cucumber
AI-driven Test Case Generation Tools	Tools for automatic test case generation	Automatically generate comprehensive test cases	TestCraft, Tricentis Tosca
		Ensure thorough test coverage	Testim, Leapwork
		Increase testing efficiency	Functionize, TestProject
		Adapt to changes in software requirements	mabl, Eggplant Functional
		Predict potential defects early	SonarQube, Parasoft
Predictive Analytics for Defect Prediction	Models for predicting defects	Proactively manage defects and mitigate risks	Kiuwan, DeepCode
		Prioritize testing efforts and allocate resources	CodeSonar, Veracode
Machine Learning Algorithms	Frameworks for machine learning algorithms	Improve accuracy and effectiveness of testing processes	TensorFlow, Scikit-learn
		Analyse data patterns and trends to make intelligent decisions	Keras, PyTorch
		Enhance decision making and optimize performance	XGBoost, LightGBM

Tool/Framework	Description	Usability in Quality Engineering	Examples(s)
Natural Language Processing (NLP)	Tools for processing natural language data	Improve communication and collaboration among teams	IBM Watson NLU, Google Cloud NLP
		Enhance requirements analysis and test case generation	NLTK, SpaCy
		Automate documentation and reporting tasks	IBM Watson, BERT, GPT-3
Generative AI	Models that generate data or content	Enhance test data generation	IBM Watson, GPT-3, GPT -4, BERT
		Automate documentation and reporting tasks	Watson.ai, Watson.data, Watson.gov, OpenAI Codex, OpenAI DALL-E

Table 6.1: AI enabled tools for QE

Below are the latest available Gen AI solutions for Quality Engineering:

- Unstructured Test Data Generation: Unstructured Test Data Generation learns from the data patterns from the training data and simulated synthetic unstructured text data from the same.

- Language-Model-Based Data Augmentation (LAMBADA) generates new sentences, then filters that content using a classifier trained on the original data. This solution uses GPT3 technology.

- Features and benefits: Here are the features and benefits in the discussion:

- Creates tests to perform positive and negative testing to support different test requirements- e.g., regression testing.

- Provides API test coverage with tests for all endpoints and end point sequences.

- Covers producer-consumer dependencies and tests for integrity of the relationship.

- Generates BDD step files that can be ingested / used by a standard Cypress or Rest Assure framework.

Identified Use-Cases

The following use cases have been identified as potential candidates for benefits realization in the near future, aligning with the vision of a AI-powered Quality Engineering practice portfolio.

Use Cases	Need for the Use Case	Benefits of the Solution	Proof Points (Client Engagements)
Improve and standardize test strategy and test planning with AI-based requirements complexity analysis to provide insights on complex test needs and test sequencing.	Complex requirements tested late can potentially delay identification of high severity defects. Lack of structured approach to identify corelated requirements.	100% early prioritization of critical components Early identification of code defects 10-15% optimization of test cases by combining testing of corelated requirements. 100% compliance to schedule adherence.	US based Retail shoe company. UK Based Building Society.
Identify and eliminate ambiguous requirements to Improve requirements quality and test design quality	Ambiguous requirements lead to poorly written tests and delays in test case design. Ambiguous requirements can result in schedule adherence and cost overrun.	100% elimination of ambiguous requirements. Improved quality of tests Better chances of meeting test schedules.	US based Retail shoe company. UK Based Building Society.
Rapidly analyse existing testbeds. Generate meaningful test models from existing test cases and eliminate duplicate test cases.	Maintaining huge repositories of test cases is cumbersome. New test cases are simply changes in the inputs data combinations, leading to more redundancy in the tests	100% Elimination of duplicate test cases results in 10-15% reduction in test cases executed. Grouping of homogeneous test cases to enable model-based testing simpler.	Large US Retail client. Australian Power Company.

Use Cases	Need for the Use Case	Benefits of the Solution	Proof Points (Client Engagements)
Evaluate huge data volumes and improve quality of the structured datasets for AI/ML Model development	Quality of data supplied to train and test AI/ML models is traditionally not been measured / evaluated consistently. Maximum AI/ML solutions fail in production due issues in the input's quality data	Standardized metrics for data quality assessment. Metrics are based on the modality of the input data. Metrics-based insights enable understanding of the quality and remediation of the datasets.	
Assess and standardize the quality of unstructured data for AI/ML solutions with standardized end-to-end metrics and models	Evaluating the quality of unstructured data inputs has always been a challenge. Businesses do not understand why the quality of data is perceived as poor. Clients do not understand if the data is skewed towards certain data combinations	Standardized metrics for data quality assessment based on modality of the input data. Easy to understand metrics-based assessment of data quality standardizes data insights. Easy to use solution provides understandable inputs through visualization of metrics consistently.	US Based Law Department.
Improve test data quality (primarily for AI/ML and data-based solutions). Remediate and manage datasets with auditable actions and based on traceable recommendations and metrics-driven insights.	There is no standardized universal way to improve the quality of the data. It is difficult to know if the data is biased, and it is tougher to normalize the data that is biased	Identification of root cause and providing remediation steps to improve the data quality for each metric helps improve the over data quality. The solution improves the data and thereby will improve the predictability of the AI/ML solutions.	US Based Law Department.

Use Cases	Need for the Use Case	Benefits of the Solution	Proof Points (Client Engagements)
Develop comprehensive test cases for unstructured datasets by intelligent representation of unstructured data as structured features to provide coverage and consistency of test cases.	Test coverage of AI/ML solution is not quantified and traditionally ignored. Coverage is based on expertise and data scientist's or business' inputs. The testing team does not understand if they have achieved sufficient test coverage from the test cases identified. Clients do not know if the unstructured data provided is biased.	Ability to create test coverage matrix using points of variations using structured representation of unstructured data. Ability to achieve 100% test coverage with optimal test combinations. Ability to provide test case recommendations to improve test coverage for Ai/ML solutions	US Based Law Department Large US Bank
Improve test and training data sets, by enhancing the data via automated data generation to address the gaps. Analyse data split densities and improve test data sets	Testers do not know if they have sufficient test data available to test every data combination supplied to AI/ML model for training. Equivalence partitioning and boundary testing is difficult for AI/ML data sets	Density-balanced data splits ensures test data sufficiently represents every data combination and provides insights to identify underperforming data combinations. The automated analysis guides and directs the tester to create tests to cover the datasets and enables the tester to ask for or create more data for testing	US Based Law Department Large US Bank

Use Cases	Need for the Use Case	Benefits of the Solution	Proof Points (Client Engagements)
Assess the Ai/ML models for fairness and consistent behavior.	Accuracy and statistical evaluation of AI/ML model is not sufficient to guarantee performance in production. Many AI/ML solutions fail in production due to inconsistent prediction of the outcome. • The solutions are very sensitive to minor changes.	Sensitivity evaluates the vulnerability of the model towards changes in input. Model performance is validated for minor and larger changes in the input data. Automated generation of test data sets validates model flip-rates	UK based Large Telecom company. US Based Law Department
Generate unstructured data synthetically based on data available.	In AI/ML applications, generating unstructured data synthetically for under-represented data combinations is a challenge.	Synthetically generated data by learning from data patterns can help normalizing biased data.	
Generate unstructured datasets that resemble a small sample set to intensively test AI/ML solutions (e.g. chatbots)	Test sets created are either not intelligently / correct English. Variations are created by extrapolating and flipping tense, including superlatives etc., which might not make sense	Using unique algorithms for Generative Pre-trained Transformer large volumes of very realistic conversations can be created by the tester. Small sample sets can be extrapolated and developed into comprehensive datasets for Chat bot testing	Large Telecom company US Based Law Department
Identify defect root cause and assign root causes by application in real time as soon as the defect is raised.	Lots of time spent on defect triage to evaluate the root cause of the defect. Assignment of the defect to an incorrect team/team member delays the resolution turnaround time.	60-70% reduction in defect triage effort spent by multiple stakeholders. 30% reduction in number of defects assigned to incorrect team/team member.	Large Latin American Telecom company. Large US based Telecom company US based Healthcare client

Use Cases	Need for the Use Case	Benefits of the Solution	Proof Points (Client Engagements)
Ability to foresee the defect patterns for the current release.	Most of the time the team takes a knee-jerk reaction to defect inflow. Resource planning and allocation has been an issue.	Defect inflow pattern can enable better resource planning.	Large Latin American Telecom company. Large US based Telecom company US based Healthcare client
Provide early insights from the defect's patterns of the current release and recommendations for course correction from the same.	This process is a post-mortem of defects after the release. Recommendations are either not implemented or not relevant for future releases.	Real-time defect analytics and recommendation implementation in current Agile sprint. AI based root cause and impacted application sights can eliminate defect triage process or simplify it. Defect inflow pattern can enable better resource planning.	Large Latin American Telecom company. Large US based Telecom company US based Healthcare client
An ability to get insights from test results to identify underperforming test scenarios and root causes for the same	Identification of under-performing test combination is a cumbersome process. Associating a root cause for the same is a challenge. Most of the time this is a speculative approach.	Ease of identification of underperforming data combinations. Association of underperforming data combinations and their representation during AI/ML training phase to provide more insights.	US Based Law Department Large US Bank

Table 6.2: Identified Use-Cases

Note: Solutions to the use cases described above are enabled on the Quality Platform. They are automated solutions that enable testers to derive rapid insights, tests, and data as the case maybe to improve the test throughput, reduce effort and standardize the test work-products. Solution applies to and across traditional software applications and AI Infused Applications and autonomous systems.

The AI Advantage

As technology continues to evolve, the adoption of Artificial Intelligence (AI) in quality engineering has become increasingly prevalent, offering both significant benefits and notable challenges. Understanding these aspects is essential for organizations seeking to leverage AI to enhance their quality engineering practices.

Benefits

The introduction of AI in Quality Engineering has transformed the way we approach testing and quality assurance, bringing numerous benefits that enhance efficiency, accuracy, and overall software quality.

- **Improved Efficiency**: AI automates repetitive tasks such as test case generation, execution, and analysis, leading to faster testing cycles and increased productivity. By reducing manual effort, QA teams can focus on more strategic and value-added activities.

- **Enhanced Accuracy**: AI-powered tools leverage advanced algorithms to analyze data and identify patterns, enabling more accurate defect detection, prediction, and analysis. This results in higher-quality software products and improved customer satisfaction.

- **Increased Test Coverage**: AI-based test case generation tools can automatically create comprehensive test suites, covering a broader range of scenarios and edge cases than manual methods. This leads to more thorough testing and better overall software quality.

- **Predictive Analytics**: AI enables predictive analytics, allowing QA teams to anticipate potential quality issues and performance bottlenecks before they occur. By leveraging historical data and machine learning algorithms, organizations can proactively address issues and optimize their processes.

- **Continuous Improvement**: AI facilitates continuous improvement by providing actionable insights derived from data analysis. By identifying trends, patterns, and areas for optimization, organizations can iteratively enhance their quality engineering practices and deliver better software products.

Challenges

As organizations embark on the journey to adopt AI in Quality Engineering, they are confronted with a range of challenges that can hinder the successful integration of AI-driven tools and frameworks into their existing processes. From ensuring data quality and availability to addressing concerns around interpretability, trust, integration complexity, ethical considerations, and skill gaps, organizations must navigate these obstacles to reap the benefits of AI-powered quality engineering.

- **Data Quality and Availability**: AI models require high-quality and representative data for training and analysis. Ensuring data quality and availability can be challenging, particularly in organizations with disparate data sources and legacy systems.

- **Interpretability and Trust**: The complexity of AI algorithms can make them difficult to interpret, leading to concerns about transparency and trust. Organizations must ensure that AI-driven decisions are explainable and understandable to stakeholders.

- **Integration Complexity**: Integrating AI-based tools and frameworks into existing quality engineering processes may require significant organizational changes, technical expertise, and collaboration across teams. Ensuring seamless integration without disrupting existing workflows can be a complex endeavor.

- **Ethical and Regulatory Considerations**: AI adoption raises ethical and regulatory considerations related to data privacy, bias and fairness. Organizations must adhere to ethical guidelines and regulatory requirements to mitigate risks and ensure responsible AI usage.

- **Skill Gap**: Adopting AI in quality engineering requires specialized skills in data science, machine learning and AI technologies. Bridging the skill gap and upskilling the existing workforce may pose challenges for organizations transitioning to AI-driven quality engineering practices.

In conclusion, while AI adoption in quality engineering offers numerous benefits, including improved efficiency, accuracy, and predictive capabilities, organizations must also navigate challenges related to data quality, interpretability, integration, ethics, and skills. By addressing these challenges proactively and leveraging AI responsibly, organizations can unlock the full potential of AI to enhance their quality engineering practices and deliver high-quality software products to customers.

Having said that, here is the focus of Quality Engineering to align technology roadmaps and indicators with the key QE imperatives/ There are 3 core areas we have invested in and focused test solution development around. Using key inputs of requirements / user stories, testcases, and defects we build tests and data for coverage across all layers of the application.

Conclusion

In this chapter, we delved into the transformative role of Artificial Intelligence (AI) in enhancing Quality Engineering (QE) practices. Building upon our understanding of AI systems and their components from the previous chapter, we shifted our focus to the practical applications and integration of AI in QE processes. Let's summarize the key takeaways. AI's infusion into quality engineering optimizes various activities, significantly augmenting human capabilities. By leveraging AI-powered tools and technologies, various activities, significantly augmenting human capabilities. By leveraging AI-powered tools and technologies, quality engineers can automate repetitive and time-consuming tasks, such as test case generation and execution, synthetic test data creation, and defect management. These tools harness machine learning algorithms to intelligently identify patterns in application behavior, enabling the generation of robust test cases that cover a wide range of scenarios and edge cases. AI-based virtual assistants and chatbots further augment QE by providing real-time assistance and guidance, streamlining workflows, and enabling informed decision-making. AI-driven test case generation involves the automatic creation of comprehensive test cases based on various inputs, significantly reducing manual effort and improving test coverage. Machine learning algorithms analyze application behavior to generate test cases that target specific functionalities and scenarios. Additionally, AI-powered test data generation tools create diverse and representative test data sets, ensuring thorough test coverage and reducing reliance on manual data creation. Defect prediction models leverage historical data to identify potential quality issues, enabling proactive defect management and risk mitigation. These models analyze patterns and trends to predict the likelihood of defects, helping QE teams prioritize testing efforts and allocate resources more effectively. The integration of AI-based tools and frameworks into the quality engineering process enhances efficiency and scalability. AI-driven test automation frameworks streamline testing processes, reduce manual intervention, and accelerate the delivery of high-quality software products. These frameworks adapt to changes in application behavior, automatically update test scripts, and identify and resolve test failures in real-time. Beyond functional testing, AI applications extend automation to performance, security, and accessibility testing, enhancing overall quality and reliability. However, integration comes with challenges such as ensuring data quality, interpretability, and seamless incorporation into existing workflows. Best practices include starting small, fostering collaboration, investing in data quality initiatives, and emphasizing transparency and explainability. Adopting AI in quality engineering offers numerous benefits, including improved efficiency, enhanced accuracy, increased test coverage, predictive analytics, and continuous improvement. Automation of repetitive tasks allows QE teams to focus on strategic analytics, and continuous improvement. Automation of repetitive tasks allows QE teams to focus on strategic activities, leading to faster delivery of high-quality software products. AI's data-driven insights reduce human error, improve defect detection, and enable proactive issue resolution. However, organizations must address challenges related to data quality, interpretability, integration complexity, ethical considerations, and skill gaps. Ensuring high-quality data, fostering trust through explainability, managing integration efforts, adhering to ethical guidelines, and upskilling the workforce are crucial for successful AI adoption. Throughout the chapter, we discussed practical examples and use cases of AI applications in quality engineering. These included AI-powered tools for test case management, test data generation, defect prediction, and test automation. Examples such as AI

Testing Asset for Test Case Management, AI Testing Asset for Test Case Execution such as AI Testing Asset for Test Case Management, AI Testing Asset for Test Case Execution, and AI-Defect Analytics and Prediction demonstrated the tangible benefits of AI in optimizing QE processes. We also explored advanced solutions like unstructured test data generation, language-model-based data augmentation, and predictive analytics for defect management.

These examples highlighted AI's potential to improve efficiency, accuracy, and overall software quality. In conclusion, AI's adoption in quality engineering offers transformative benefits, including improved efficiency, accuracy, predictive capabilities, and continuous improvement. By leveraging AI-powered tools and frameworks, organizations can automate repetitive tasks, enhance test coverage, and proactively address quality issues. However, successful AI adoption requires addressing challenges related to data quality, interpretability, integration complexity, ethics, and skills. By embracing best practices and leveraging AI responsibly, organizations can unlock the full potential of AI to enhance their quality engineering practices and deliver high-quality software products to customers. As we move forward, the focus of Quality Engineering will be to align technology roadmaps and indicators with key QE imperatives. Investing in AI-driven solutions and focusing on test solution development around requirements, user stories, test cases, and defects will enable comprehensive test coverage and continuous improvement across all layers of the application.

In the next chapter, we will be discussing how generative AI technology has changed quality engineering practices and the role of quality engineer in detail.

Exercise: Test Your Understanding

Answer the following questions and test your understanding of learning from Chapter 6:

Q. 1. What is one key focus area of AI in quality engineering?

    A. Manual testing optimization

    B. Synthetic test data generation

    X. Hardware integration testing

    Δ. Data storage optimization

Q. 2. Which of the following is a benefit of integrating AI-based tools into the quality engineering process?

    A. Increased dependency on manual intervention

    B. Improved efficiency and accuracy in testing

    C. Elimination of all testing frameworks

    D. Reduced need for defect management

Q. 3. What is a major challenge of adopting AI in quality engineering?

A.   The inability to automate test case generation

B.   Limited scalability of AI frameworks

C.   Integration of AI tools into existing processes

D.   Lack of interest in quality engineering practices

Q. 4. How can AI improve defect management in quality engineering?

A.   By automating the identification and prioritization of defects

B.   By increasing the number of defects identified manually

C.   By eliminating the need for defect tracking systems

D.   By generating synthetic test data

Q. 5. What is an effective approach to overcoming challenges in adopting AI for quality engineering

E.   Avoiding the use of AI for critical testing tasks

A.   Developing a comprehensive strategy for AI integration

B.   Relying solely on AI for all quality engineering activities

C.   Using traditional methods alongside AI without integration

Chapter 7

Generative AI and It's Role in Quality Engineering

As we witness the rapid progression of technology, the realm of Quality Engineering arrives at a crucial juncture where the incorporation of state-of-the-art artificial intelligence methodologies, specifically Generative AI, known as GenAI, becomes essential. In this chapter, we set forth on an expedition to examine the significant influence of Generative AI (GenAI) on Quality Engineering, highlighting three primary elements that will define the future of software and product quality assurance. We will investigate the core principles of Generative AI and its impact on quality engineering, providing insight that transcends the superficial level.

In addition, we will traverse the pragmatic landscape of utilizing generative AI methods for test case creation and diversification, revealing the transformative capacity of these technologies in refining testing procedures. Moreover, we will discuss the ethical concerns and obstacles related to the incorporation of generative AI in quality engineering, ensuring that conscientious and deliberate practices align with the quest for innovation. Join us in uncovering the connection between Generative AI and Quality Engineering, where ingenuity and accountability unite to sculpt the future of software testing and product quality assurance.

In this chapter, we will discuss the following topics:

- Grasping generative AI and its ramifications on quality engineering.
- Employing generative AI approaches for test case production and variety.
- Ethical Considerations and Challenges Pertaining to Generative AI in Quality Engineering.

Understanding generative AI and its impact on quality engineering

Generative AI will significantly influence the quality engineering design, implementation, and reporting phases where quality engineers create and design content in the form of requirement analysis, test strategies, test plans, test case design and maintenance (manual/automated), code migration between testing tools, test execution result capture, test reporting, defect management, defect root cause analysis and test KPI measurement.

Test data identification will be crucial in Generative AI, concerning data quality, ethical considerations, model interpretation, security, and privacy.

Generative AI acts as a transformative power in Quality Engineering, redefining conventional testing approaches. Its capability to autonomously generate relevant data, test cases, and diverse situations revolutionizes the Quality Engineering field. As discussed in previous chapters, Generative AI is not merely a tool but an innovation catalyst, expanding the horizons of what is attainable in software testing.

One of the essential contributions of Generative AI to Quality Engineering is its function in automating test case creation. By comprehending the complexities of requirements and application functionalities, Generative AI can rapidly generate comprehensive test cases, lessening the manual effort needed for this vital aspect of testing. Furthermore, its capacity to incorporate diversity in generated test cases ensures a more rigorous evaluation of the application under examination.

In the subsequent section, we have outlined some potential areas that can be easily explored to enable the integration of Generative AI into Quality Engineering.

Leveraging generative AI techniques for test case generation and diversity

This chapter delves into the influential effects of generative AI methods on test case creation and diversity within software testing. We commence with an in-depth examination of practical applications in test case generation; the discussion then proceeds to clarify the criteria and factors for choosing suitable testing tools, underlining the role of AI in making well-informed decisions tailored to specific use cases. The notion of domain-agnostic testing is investigated, demonstrating how generative AI offers indispensable guidance across various domains, ensuring adaptability and scalability in testing practices. The chapter further scrutinizes the inventive application of AI in converting written comments into functional code and the role of models such as CodeGPT in refactoring code for enhanced testability. It also highlights how generative AI assists in automatically generating explanations for test automation code, pinpointing and resolving problems, optimizing code for efficiency improvements, and enabling code conversion between distinct testing frameworks. The chapter concludes by accentuating the vital role of generative AI in delivering comprehensive support for the testing lifecycle and addressing the importance of risk analysis in this evolving environment.

GenAI Use cases in Quality Engineering: A Roadmap to Efficiency

In the realm of Quality Engineering (QE) lifecycle, Generative AI (GenAI) introduces a spectrum of innovative use cases that redefine efficiency, collaboration, and decision-making. Organized under Garage Methods, these GenAI-driven applications span across the entire QE lifecycle, providing unprecedented advancements.

Planning

GenAI revolutionizes the planning phase by introducing automation and intelligence to critical activities:

- **Test Plan Sequencing and Dependency Analysis**: GenAI dynamically sequences test cases based on dependencies, enabling the creation of efficient and streamlined test plans.

- **QE Acceptance Criteria and Test Scenario Generation**: By generating acceptance criteria and test scenarios, GenAI simplifies the planning process and ensures thorough coverage.

- **Test Plan Design and Documentation (ARD)**: Automated design and documentation of test plans ensure accuracy and save time, enabling teams to focus on critical tasks.

Co-Create

Leveraging GenAI's capabilities, teams can enhance collaboration and test creation:

- **CTD Model Attributes and Values**: GenAI extracts attributes and values from requirement documents to create Combinatorial Test Design (CTD) models.

- **Mainframe Testing Automation**: Automates test case generation and execution for mainframe applications, reducing complexity and improving accuracy.

- **Automatic Test Scenario Creation**: GenAI generates test scenarios for CRM systems like Salesforce/Einstein and SAP, enhancing testing for complex workflows.

- **Test Case Creation through Requirement/Code Analysis**: GenAI analyzes requirements and code to automatically generate test cases, ensuring precision and efficiency.

Co-Execute

GenAI transforms the execution phase by improving efficiency and adaptability:

- **BDD Test Script Generation**: Utilizes Behavior-Driven Development (BDD) principles to create test scripts aligned with user behaviors.

- **Test Data Generation from Business Rules**: Automates the creation of realistic test data based on business rules for comprehensive testing.

- **Performance Test Script Generation**: Facilitates the generation of performance test scripts using tools like RPT, LoadRunner, and JMeter.

- **Self-Healing Selenium Tests**: Enhances test reliability with smart locators, reducing instability in Selenium tests.

- **Decision-Making Based on Changing Data**: Predicts required test cases by analyzing dynamic data changes and code commits.

Co-Operate

GenAI fosters collaboration and efficient communication throughout the testing lifecycle:

- **Intelligent Reporting**: AI-powered defect analysis and prediction tools deliver insightful reports.

- **End-to-End Test Assistance Bot**: A smart bot supports comprehensive testing activities, ensuring smooth workflows.

Manage

With GenAI, the management phase becomes smarter and more proactive:

- **AI-Enabled Test Status Review**: Bots analyze test statuses, code changes, and metrics to recommend which tests to execute.

- **Digital Worker Development**: Builds digital workers within Intelligent Quality Platforms (IQP) to provide Level 1 support.

Close

GenAI brings closure to the testing lifecycle with meaningful insights:

- **Productivity Reporting**: Generates detailed productivity scorecards for developers and testers, offering actionable insights to enhance quality engineering processes.

This comprehensive integration of GenAI empowers Quality Engineering teams to achieve unparalleled efficiency, accuracy, and collaboration at every stage of the testing lifecycle.

Exploring GenAI Technology: Applications in Quality Engineering

The exploration of GenAI technology in Quality Engineering reveals a groundbreaking approach to address various challenges in the field. Focusing on core testing, GenAI leverages Large Language Models (LLMs) to automate the identification and sequencing of test cases, streamlining the test planning phase. The prospective GPT solutions further extend to Natural Language Understanding, offering a more efficient means of defining acceptance criteria and generating Quality Engineering artifacts based on requirements and user stories. Content Generation plays a pivotal role, transforming static test reporting into dynamic presentations and automating the creation of Combinatorial Test Design (CTD) models, test scenarios, and execution scripts. The application of GenAI is not confined to core testing, as it extends to defect management, data quality engineering, mainframe testing, test automation, and SAP testing, showcasing its transformative potential across diverse facets of Quality Engineering.

Here's a breakdown of its transformative applications across core areas of QE:

Core Testing

Core testing forms the foundation of QE by ensuring test cases are well-structured, acceptance criteria are clear, and reports are insightful.

- **Use Case**: Dynamic Test Reporting

    Description: Test reporting becomes dynamic with GenAI, which integrates with test management tools to create tailored, real-time reports. This includes summaries of test results, coverage, and insights into potential issues.

    Solution: Content Generation transforms static reports into actionable presentations for management and teams.

- **Use Case**: Defect Management and Analytics

Description: By analyzing historical data, GenAI provides insights into defect patterns, predicts trends, and identifies test cases for re-execution. This feedback loop enhances lifecycle efficiency.

Solution: Natural Language Understanding powers these predictive and preventive insights.

- **Use Case**: Generating CTD Models and Cucumber Scenarios

Description: GenAI extracts business rules to create Combinatorial Test Design (CTD) models, attributes, and test scenarios, reducing effort while maintaining consistency.

Solution: Natural Language Understanding generates CTD artifacts and identifies impacted models.

Data Quality Engineering

Data quality ensures testing aligns with accurate, context-specific data.

- **Use Case**: Data Identification and Provisioning

Description: GenAI identifies, and provisions data required for test execution by analyzing requirements and CTD models. It ensures the accuracy of test data, aligning it with defined criteria.

Solution: Content Generation integrates Behavior-Driven Development (BDD) test cases with LLMs for precise data provisioning.

Mainframe Testing

Mainframe environments demand specialized testing approaches to address legacy systems.

- **Use Case**: CTD Test Cases and Execution Scripts

Description: GenAI simplifies mainframe testing by generating CTD test cases and automation scripts from COBOL/PL1 code and tools like ADDI. This reduces manual intervention and improves efficiency.

Solution: Content Generation accelerates script creation, aiding complex mainframe testing.

Test Automation

Automation is pivotal for scaling and consistency in testing.

- **Use Case**: Automatic Scenario and Case Creation

Description: GenAI introduces conversational agents to generate test cases by analyzing requirements or responding to natural language prompts, making automation intuitive and accessible.

Solution: Conversational Agents create scenarios and cases efficiently, enhancing automation.

SAP Testing

SAP testing addresses the unique challenges of enterprise processes.

- **Use Case**: Automatic CTD Model and Test Generation

Description: GenAI reads SAP process flows and BPMN files to generate CTD models and test cases automatically. This eliminates manual effort and enhances testing speed.

Solution: Content Generation bridges the gap between process documentation and actionable test artifacts.

Enhancing Telco Quality with GenAI: Problem-Solving Narratives

This section is designed for practitioners and researchers exploring the transformative role of generative AI in software testing. It emphasizes bridging the gap between development and testing, automating test-related tasks, and ensuring cross-domain adaptability. By leveraging Telco use cases, this chapter highlights the pivotal role of generative AI in optimizing software testing processes and driving continuous quality improvement.

Test Case Generation Use Case

We will see a couple of Use cases:

Problem Statement

In the fast-paced world of modern software development, ensuring the dependability and quality of applications hinges on efficient and effective testing processes. However, testing teams face several challenges:

- **Manual Effort**: Test case generation remains a labor-intensive task, consuming significant time and resources.

- **Complexity**: Increasing software complexity demands extensive test case coverage, which can be overwhelming.

- **Risk of Errors**: Human-generated test cases may result in incomplete coverage, allowing defects to go unnoticed.

These challenges underline the need for an automated and intelligent solution that enhances speed, precision, and coverage. Generative AI offers an innovative approach, revolutionizing test case generation and ensuring a more efficient, scalable, and reliable testing process.

GenAI-Based Solution

Generative AI addresses the limitations of manual test case generation by leveraging its ability to:

- **Understand Complex Requirements**: Using advanced natural language processing, Generative AI analyzes application features and requirements.

- **Automate Test Case Creation**: It autonomously generates diverse test cases directly from test requirements, ensuring comprehensive scenario coverage.

- **Improve Efficiency**: This approach accelerates the testing process, significantly reducing timelines while maintaining quality.

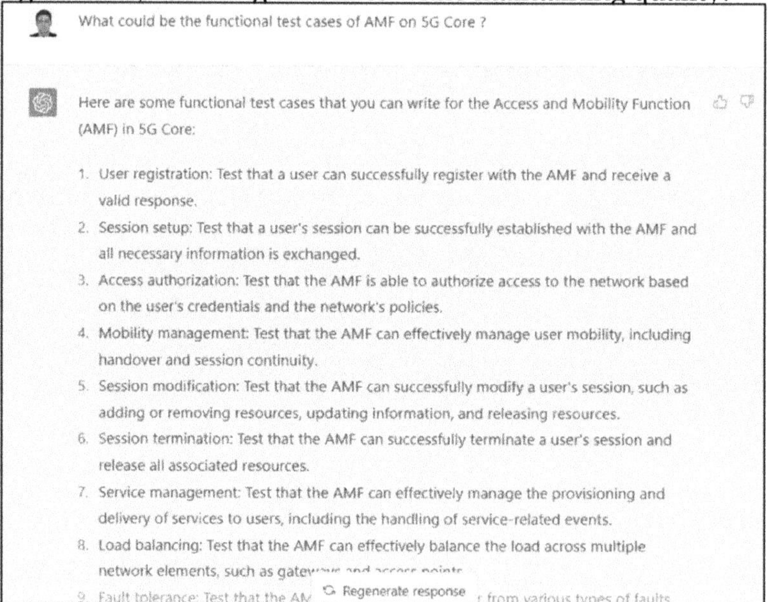

Figure 7.1: Functional test cases for AMF node on 5G Core

- **Enhance Coverage**: By identifying and addressing potential gaps in testing, it minimizes the likelihood of undetected defects.

The process of Generative AI-based test case and test data generation for Telco use cases is illustrated in the accompanying figure. This streamlined methodology ensures thorough coverage while adapting to the dynamic requirements of Telco applications, providing a robust foundation for quality assurance.

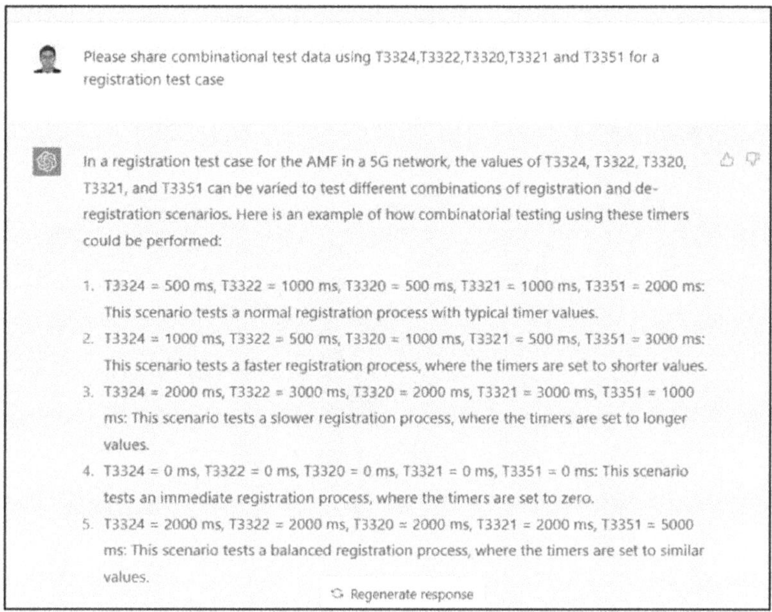

Figure 7.2: Functional test cases for AMF node on 5G Core

Test Tool Selection Use Cases

We will see a couple of Use cases:

Problem Statement

Quality Engineering teams encounter a formidable challenge in navigating the expansive landscape of testing tools to make optimal choices for their projects. The plethora of tools available, each designed to address specific testing needs, often leads to decision paralysis and the risk of suboptimal tool selection. The criticality of choosing the right testing tools is underscored by the potential impact on testing efficiency, project timelines, and overall software quality.

GenAI-Based Solution

To alleviate the complexities associated with test tool selection, Generative AI emerges as a powerful ally for Quality Engineering teams. Leveraging machine learning algorithms, Generative AI analyzes project requirements, historical data, and industry benchmarks while also considering cost implications. By synthesizing this information, it provides informed recommendations on the most suitable testing tools tailored to the unique characteristics of the project. This GenAI-driven approach ensures that Quality Engineering teams transcend decision paralysis, making strategic choices that maximize testing efficiency and overall effectiveness, ultimately contributing to the success of software development projects.

The below mentioned figure explains the process of GenAI based test data generation for a Telco Use case.

Please suggest the open source tools we can use to perform a testing project with below requirement : Functional testing of cloud native application

There are several open source tools that can be used for functional testing of cloud native applications. Here are some suggestions:

1. Selenium: Selenium is a popular open source tool for functional testing of web applications. It supports multiple programming languages and browsers, making it a versatile tool for testing cloud native applications.
2. TestNG: TestNG is a testing framework for Java applications. It provides features such as parallel testing, data-driven testing, and test configuration, making it a good choice for testing cloud native applications built on the Java stack.
3. Robot Framework: Robot Framework is a generic test automation framework that supports multiple programming languages and test libraries. It is designed to be easy to use and to support both keyword-driven and data-driven testing, making it a good choice for testing cloud native applications.
4. Cypress: Cypress is a modern web testing framework that is designed to make testing web applications easy and intuitive. It supports end-to-end testing, integration testing, and unit testing, making it a good choice for testing cloud native applications built on modern web stacks.
5. JMeter: JMeter is an open source tool for load testing, performance testing, and functional testing of web applications. It supports multiple protocols, including HTTP,

Figure 7.3: Test Data generation for AMF node on 5G Core

Test Tool Selection Use Cases

We will see a couple of Use cases:

Problem Statement

While test automation is crucial for faster and more reliable testing, the manual creation of automation scripts remains a time-intensive process. This manual effort can impede the agility of the development lifecycle.

GenAI-Based Solution

Generative AI streamlines test automation by automating the script-writing process. By understanding application flows and functionalities, it can generate automation scripts autonomously. This not only accelerates the automation process but also reduces the dependency on manual scripting, making test automation more responsive to the dynamic nature of software development. Below mentioned figure explains the process of GenAI based test automation code generation for a Telco Use case.

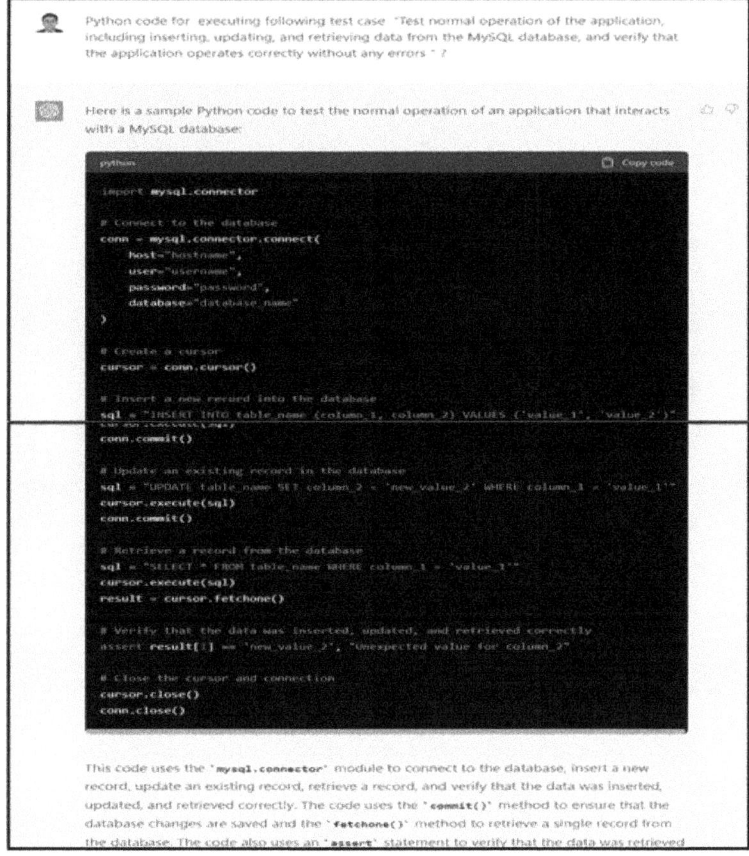

Figure 7.4: *Test automation for a Telco Use case*

This model will provide a list of test combinations when we use pair-wise testing approach. Increasing the coverage requirement will provide more test combinations.

Domain Agnostic Testing Handholding

We will see a couple of Use cases:

Problem Statement

Testing across different domains often requires different testing tools and methodologies. Adapting to new domains can be challenging, leading to a lack of consistency in testing approaches.

GenAI-Based Solution

Generative AI is inherently domain-agnostic, meaning it can adapt to new domains seamlessly. This provides a standardized testing approach that can be applied consistently across projects with different domains. The versatility of Generative AI enhances the efficiency of Quality Engineering teams working on projects spanning various industries.

Getting Functional Code from Written Comments

We will see a couple of Use cases:

Problem Statement

Understanding the functional requirements from written comments or documentation can be time-consuming and may result in misinterpretations, leading to discrepancies between the intended functionality and the implemented code.

GenAI-Based Solution

Generative AI aids in bridging the gap between documentation and code. Quality Engineering professionals can input written comments or functional requirements, and Generative AI tools, like CodeGPT, can generate corresponding functional code. This accelerates the coding process and ensures that the implemented functionality aligns closely with the intended specifications. Below mentioned figure explains the process of dealing with GenAI Code Assistant extensions with a popular IDE.

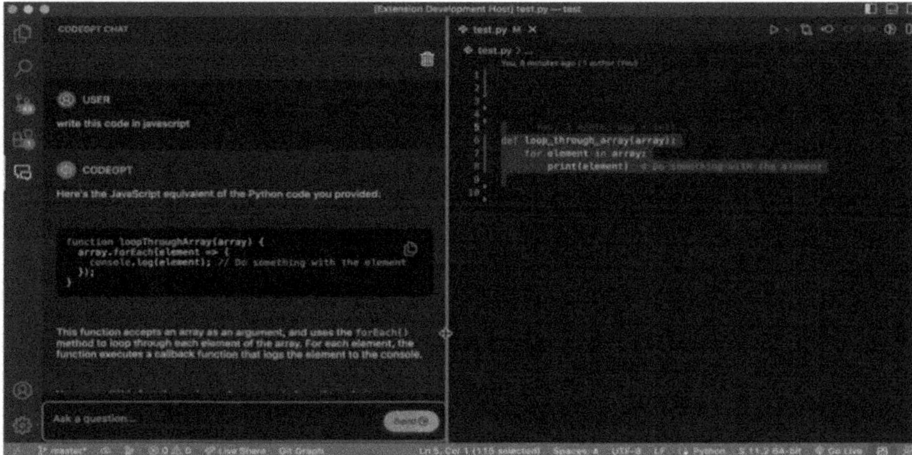

Figure 7.5: *Process of dealing with GenAI Code Assistant extensions with a popular IDE*

Refactor the Code with CodeGPT

We will see a couple of Use cases:

Problem Statement

Over time, codebases may become complex and challenging to maintain. Refactoring code to enhance readability, maintainability, and performance is a critical task that demands careful consideration.

GenAI-Based Solution

Generative AI, particularly CodeGPT, can assist in code refactoring. By understanding the existing codebase and its requirements, CodeGPT can propose refactoring suggestions. This enables Quality Engineering professionals to streamline their code, making it more efficient and maintainable without the need for extensive manual analysis. Below mentioned figure explains the process of code re-factoring with GenAI Code Assistant extensions with a popular IDE.

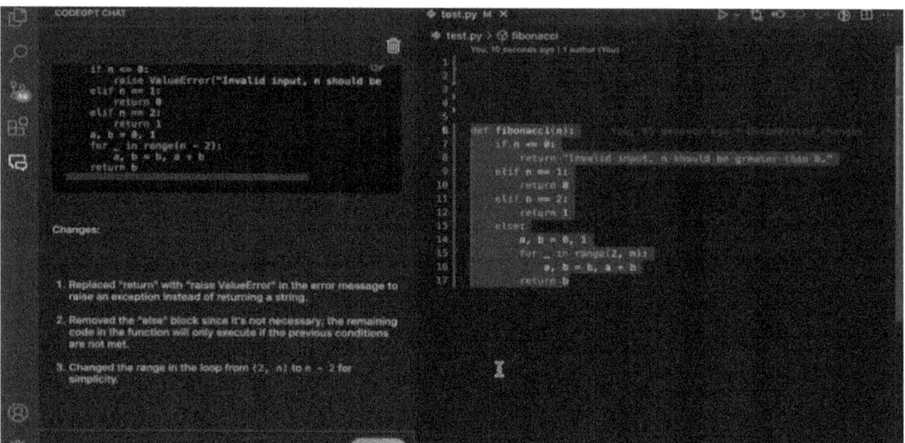

Figure 7.6: Process of code re-factoring with GenAI Code Assistant extensions with a popular IDE

Getting Test Automation Code Explanation

We will see a couple of Use cases:

Problem Statement

In the realm of Quality Engineering, the intricacies of test automation code often pose a challenge. Understanding the purpose and functionality of specific code segments is crucial for fostering effective collaboration within Quality Engineering teams. The complexity of modern software projects requires a streamlined approach to unravel the intricacies of test automation code for optimal teamwork and code comprehension.

GenAI-Based Solution

Generative AI emerges as a transformative solution for Quality Engineering professionals seeking explanations for test automation code. Through interaction with tools like CodeGPT, testers can seamlessly receive detailed explanations for code segments, enhancing their comprehension and facilitating collaboration within the team. This GenAI-driven approach not only accelerates the learning curve for team members but also promotes a deeper understanding of the test automation code's intricacies. The chapter includes a visual representation illustrating the process of code explanation with GenAI Code Assistant extensions integrated into a popular Integrated Development Environment (IDE).

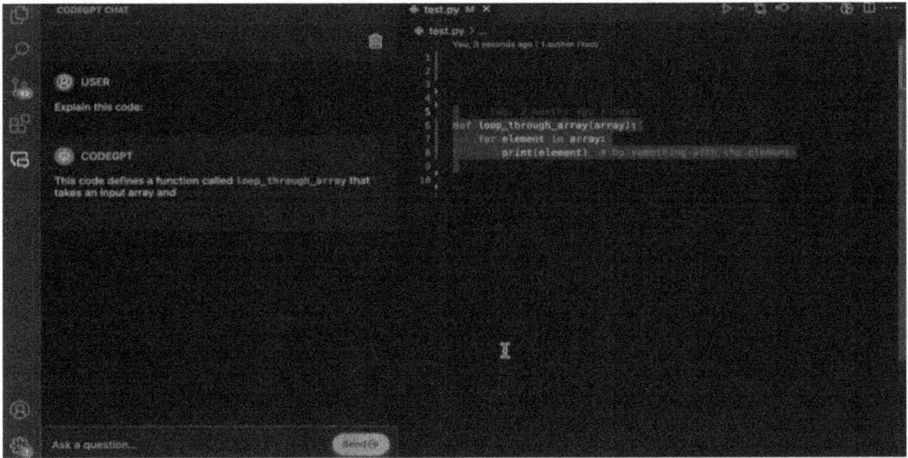

Figure 7.7: Process of code explanation with GenAI Code Assistant extensions with a popular IDE

Find a Problem on Test Automation Code

We will see a couple of Use cases:

Problem Statement

The process of identifying issues or bugs in test automation code poses a substantial challenge, particularly within extensive codebases. Manual reviews, while valuable, can be time-consuming and may inadvertently overlook subtle problems that have the potential to compromise the reliability of automated tests. As software projects grow in complexity, the need for a more efficient and comprehensive approach to problem identification in test automation code becomes increasingly evident.

GenAI-Based Solution

Generative AI offers a groundbreaking solution to the challenge of problem identification within test automation code. Leveraging tools like CodeGPT, Quality Engineering professionals can employ Generative AI to analyze code segments systematically. By doing so, it becomes possible to identify potential issues, even those that might be subtle or easily overlooked in a manual review. This GenAI-driven approach ensures the robustness of test automation suites, contributing to the overall reliability and effectiveness of the testing process.

Optimize a Piece of Test Automation Code

We will see a couple of Use cases:

Problem Statement

Test automation code optimization is crucial for enhancing execution speed and resource utilization. Manual optimization might be a daunting task, and overlooking optimization opportunities is a risk.

GenAI-Based Solution

Generative AI supports Quality Engineering professionals in optimizing test automation code. CodeGPT can suggest optimizations based on its understanding of coding best practices, leading to more efficient and performant test automation suites.

Test Automation Code Conversion Between Different Frameworks

We will see a couple of Use cases:

Problem Statement

Migration or conversion of test automation code between different frameworks poses challenges due to variations in syntax, structure, and functionalities.

Gen AI-Based Solution

Generative AI simplifies the process of code conversion between different frameworks. Quality Engineering professionals can leverage CodeGPT to automate parts of the conversion process, reducing manual effort and potential errors in adapting code to a new testing framework.

End-to-End Test Handholding

We will see a couple of Use cases:

Problem Statement

End-to-end testing involves validating the entire software system, including complex interactions between various components. Creating comprehensive end-to-end test scenarios manually can be error-prone and time-consuming.

GenAI-Based Solution

Generative AI aids in creating end-to-end test scenarios by simulating real-world interactions. It understands the intricacies of the software system and generates test cases that mimic complex user journeys. This enhances the reliability of end-to-end tests, ensuring that critical scenarios are thoroughly validated. Typical Solution

Diagram of an End-to-End Test Handling use Case of GenAI on Telco Testing.

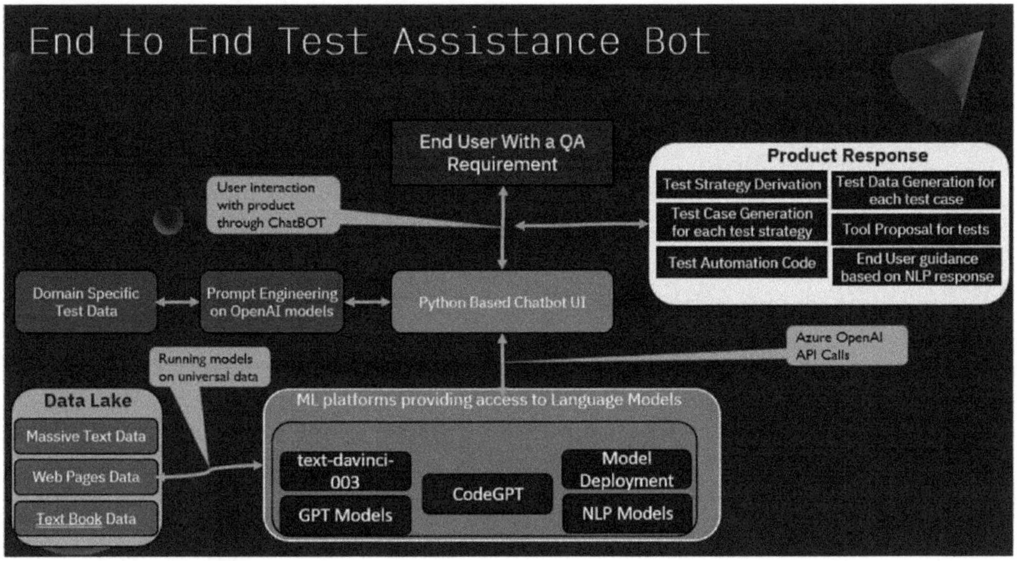

Figure 7.8: *Solution Diagram of an End-to-End Test Handling use Case of GenAI on Telco Testing*

Risk Analysis

We will see a couple of Use cases:

Problem Statement

Identifying and mitigating potential risks in software development is a crucial aspect of Quality Engineering. However, anticipating all possible risk scenarios manually can be challenging.

GenAI-Based Solution

Generative AI contributes to risk analysis by simulating diverse scenarios that might pose potential risks to the software. By autonomously generating test cases that encompass various risk factors, it enables Quality Engineering teams to proactively identify and address potential issues before they impact the production environment. This proactive approach enhances the overall quality and reliability of the software.

Having said that, the following sections highlight the promising domains where GenAI is actively contributing to the evolution of Quality Engineering practices, emphasizing its role as a catalyst for positive change in software testing methodologies.

Ethical Considerations and Challenges Related to Generative AI in Quality Engineering

As with any transformative technology, Generative AI brings forth ethical considerations and challenges. The very nature of AI, including Generative AI, raises questions about bias, privacy, and the responsible use of technology. It becomes imperative for organizations to establish guidelines and frameworks that ensure the ethical deployment of Generative AI in Quality Engineering.

Addressing Bias and Fairness

Biases in training data can lead to biased models, impacting the fairness of generated test cases. Ethical considerations include addressing and mitigating these biases, ensuring that testing practices are not inadvertently discriminatory. Transparent and fair AI practices are essential for maintaining the integrity of the testing process.

Data Privacy Concerns

Generative AI often relies on vast datasets to learn and generate meaningful content. However, the use of sensitive data raises concerns about privacy. Organizations must prioritize data protection measures, ensuring that Generative AI processes adhere to privacy regulations and standards.

Ensuring Responsible AI Practices

The conscientious implementation of Generative AI in Quality Engineering necessitates the formulation of guidelines for its application, encompassing routine audits, transparency in decision-making processes, and continuous assessment of Generative AI's influence on testing practices. Organizations must exhibit dedication to preserving ethical standards when incorporating AI technologies.

As we wrap up this investigation of Generative AI in Quality Engineering, it becomes apparent that this technology possesses immense potential for the future of software testing. The collaboration between Generative AI and Quality Engineering is set to enhance efficiency, precision, and variety of testing practices. Nonetheless, a prudent approach is vital to address the ethical considerations and challenges, ensuring that the integration of Generative AI adheres to the principles of responsible and fair testing. The journey persists as we look forward to additional innovations and breakthroughs in the ever-evolving realm of Generative AI in Quality Engineering.

Conclusion

In conclusion, the integration of Generative AI into Quality Engineering represents a significant milestone in the evolution of software testing and product quality assurance. As technology advances rapidly, the collaboration between Generative

AI and Quality Engineering is set to redefine the testing landscape by enhancing efficiency, accuracy, and diversity in test case generation and optimization. The transformative potential of Generative AI goes beyond automating test case creation; it also addresses challenges in tool selection, test automation, domain-agnostic testing, code refactoring, and risk analysis. By automating these processes, Generative AI reduces manual effort, minimizes human error, and ensures comprehensive coverage of test scenarios, ultimately leading to higher-quality software applications. However, the successful adoption of Generative AI in Quality Engineering requires a thoughtful approach to navigate the ethical considerations and challenges associated with this powerful technology. Organizations must prioritize addressing bias and fairness in AI models, ensuring data privacy, and promoting responsible AI practices. By establishing guidelines and frameworks for the ethical deployment of Generative AI, organizations can maintain the integrity of the testing process and uphold the principles of responsible and equitable testing. In the coming years, Generative AI will continue to play a crucial role in shaping the future of Quality Engineering. As new innovations and advancements emerge in the realm of Generative AI, Quality Engineering professionals must stay current with the latest developments to harness the technology's full potential. This includes participating in ongoing education, training, and industry collaboration to ensure that the benefits of Generative AI are shared widely and accessible to all stakeholders in the software development lifecycle.

Moreover, it is essential for organizations to foster a culture of continuous improvement and innovation, where the adoption of Generative AI is seen not as a one-time event but as a catalyst for the ongoing transformation of Quality Engineering practices. This mindset encourages teams to experiment, iterate, and learn from both successes and failures, fostering a more agile and resilient approach to software testing that is better equipped to navigate the challenges and opportunities of the digital era.

Ultimately, the journey of Generative AI in Quality Engineering is still in its early stages, and there is much to explore and discover in the years ahead. By embracing the power of Generative AI and addressing ethical considerations and challenges, organizations can unlock unprecedented opportunities to enhance software testing and product quality assurance. Looking to the future, the synergy between Generative AI and Quality Engineering will continue to play a pivotal role in shaping the software development landscape, ensuring that the quest for innovation and excellence remains at the heart of technological progress.

Exercise: Test Your Understanding

Answer the following questions and test your understanding of learning from Chapter 7:

Q. 1. Which of the following is a key contribution of Generative AI to Quality Engineering?

  A. Increasing manual effort in test case creation

  B. Reducing test coverage

  X. Automating test case generation

  Δ. Slowing down the testing process

Q. 2. What is a major challenge associated with manual test case generation?

  A. Incomplete test coverage

  B. High efficiency

  C. Low resource utilization

  D. Rapid execution

Q. 3. Which of the following ethical considerations is crucial in Generative AI implementation in Quality Engineering?

  A. Ignoring data privacy concerns

  B. Promoting biased models

  C. Ensuring responsible AI practices

  D. Avoiding transparency

Q. 4. Which Generative AI technique can assist in code refactoring for improved testability?

  A. Content Generation

  B. Natural Language Understanding

  C. CodeGPT

  D. Conversational Agents

Q. 5. In the context of Generative AI in Quality Engineering, what does domain-agnostic testing refer to?

  A. Testing limited to a specific domain

  B. Inability to adapt to new domains

  C. A standardized testing approach applicable across diverse domains

  D. Testing that focuses only on domain-specific features

Chapter 8

AI-based Application Testing and Reporting

In the chapters leading up to this one, we have discussed various aspects of testing AI-infused applications. We covered the need to validate the quality of these probabilistic applications, the methods for evaluating the quality of each component of these systems, and the statistical approaches used for the evaluation.

This chapter brings all of these concepts together to present a holistic approach to testing AI systems. It focuses on consolidating the various aspects of testing these systems and the best practices for doing so.

In this chapter, we will discuss the following topics:

- A comprehensive overview of the various methodologies and approaches employed in the realm of AI-focused application testing, which are designed to optimize and streamline the process of evaluating software performance and functionality.

- The strategic utilization of AI technology to significantly enhance test execution and prioritization, ensuring that critical issues are identified and resolved in a timely and efficient manner, thereby improving the overall quality and reliability of the application under examination.

- The importance of effectively conveying and presenting the results and findings of AI-fueled assessments at every stage of the delivery process, with an emphasis on clear communication and data-driven insights, to enable informed decision-making and facilitate seamless collaboration among stakeholders.

- A compilation of top strategies and best practices for conducting successful AI testing, gleaned from the experience of industry experts and thought leaders, which can serve as valuable guidance for professionals seeking to harness the power of AI to optimize their testing workflows and achieve better outcomes.

Introduction to approaches in testing AI-based applications

This section explores the crucial role of data quality and thorough testing in the development of AI applications. It starts by highlighting the importance of data quality, outlining methods for assessing data completeness and identifying biases. Next, it examines various testing methodologies, including model-based testing and test data generation. The section then addresses the challenges of evaluating AI components and emphasizes the need for automated end-to-end testing to ensure the reliability and consistency of AI systems.

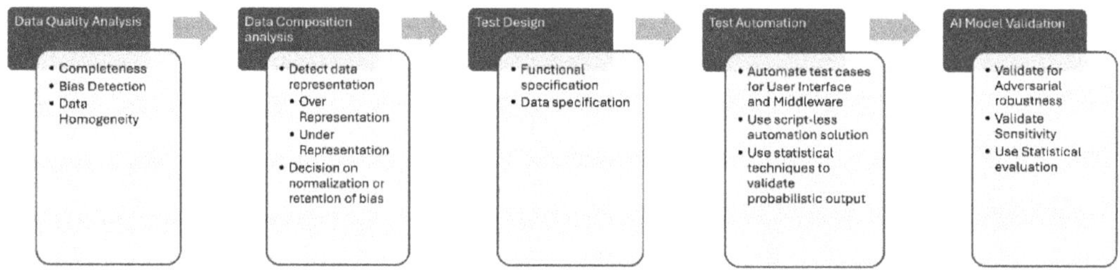

Figure 8.1: Generic Solution

The success of AI applications heavily depends on the quality of the data they are trained on. Data quality assessment plays a pivotal role in ensuring that AI systems learn effectively and produce accurate results. This section explores the importance of data quality, the methods used for evaluation, and the various testing techniques required to ensure comprehensive and unbiased data for AI systems.

Data Quality Assessment

In AI applications, the significance of data quality cannot be overstated. It is essential to identify missing or incomplete data, where information may be present for certain parameters but absent for others within the same data set. These inconsistencies can result in skewed or inaccurate learning, which could lead to failed solutions. Addressing concerns about the sufficiency of business scenarios in training data and identifying potential biases is critical. Evaluating data quality through a data science lens is vital to improving the predictability and reliability of machine learning components. Techniques such as metrics-based analysis and data split analysis help assess data completeness and identify biases, ensuring a more reliable learning process.

Data Testing Methods

AI applications require testing methods capable of evaluating the sensitivity and distribution of input data. These methods help ensure that the data aligns with real-time patterns and supports accurate decision-making. Key techniques include retaining data for real-time simulation, normalizing data through synthetic data generation, and performing combinatorial testing for sufficiency. Additionally, evaluating the sparseness of data in underrepresented clusters ensures that all data combinations are represented, providing comprehensive testing coverage.

Test Design Using Model-Based Testing Approach

Creating an effective test design for AI-infused applications relies on key inputs, such as functional specifications, and an understanding of the data's role in the process. By profiling data and analyzing data buckets, critical insights into lexical diversity and data combinations can be obtained. The model-based testing approach, particularly Combinatorial Test Design (CTD), utilizes mathematical models to identify points of variation and generate test scenarios with maximum coverage, ensuring that the AI system is thoroughly tested.

Points of Variation

Identifying features for machine learning (ML) model creation and categorizing data combinations based on these features is a key aspect of test design. Ensuring that the data representation aligns with real-time patterns is essential for generating meaningful test combinations, which results in more effective testing of AI models.

Enhancing Test Design with Data Insights

Data provisioning for AI application testing requires reflecting real-time patterns in data representation. Ensuring data variation helps evaluate consistent AI behavior while adhering to data quality metrics. In cases where sufficient data points are unavailable, synthetic data generation becomes essential to maintain testing integrity and robustness.

Test Data Generation

Both manual and automated approaches for generating test data play crucial roles in ensuring comprehensive testing of AI systems. AI-driven techniques for generating synthetic unstructured text, images, and audio data provide valuable support in testing diverse scenarios. It is essential to ensure that generated test data meets established quality metrics, ensuring that AI models are tested under realistic conditions.

AI Model Evaluation

In this section, we will explore AI Model Evaluation:

Evaluating AI Components

Traditional unit testing methods struggle to evaluate AI and machine learning (ML) components due to their probabilistic nature. To overcome these challenges, probability-based evaluation, statistical analysis using large datasets, and API-level testing are necessary for a more comprehensive evaluation of AI components. These approaches ensure that AI systems are assessed thoroughly, considering their inherent uncertainties.

Consistency of Results

Achieving consistency in AI or ML component outputs is crucial for ensuring reliable performance. Evaluating the sensitivity and inconsistency of these components helps determine their reliability and predictability over time, which is essential for maintaining high standards of performance in AI applications.

End-to-End Application Testing

To fully assess AI systems, it's essential to evaluate their user interface against requirements. By treating AI/ML components as black-box entities, automated end-to-end testing can be performed for regression and integration purposes. This approach integrates testing into the DevOps pipeline, streamlining the testing process and enhancing overall efficiency.

Test Results Evaluation

Evaluating expected test results is a critical component of the end-to-end testing process. Considering time and cost implications, particularly when dealing with large datasets, emphasizes the importance of efficiency in testing. Streamlining the process through automation ensures that testing is both effective and cost-efficient.

Testing AI-infused applications requires a meticulous approach to evaluating data quality, designing comprehensive test cases, and effectively testing models and components. The integration of AI-specific testing techniques, such as probabilistic evaluation and model-based testing, ensures a robust evaluation process that enhances the predictability and reliability of AI systems. Automated testing practices further streamline the testing process, making it a crucial aspect of the software development lifecycle and ensuring the overall success of AI applications.

Leveraging AI for intelligent test execution and prioritization

Navigating the complex landscape of AI-infused applications, Quality Engineers play a pivotal role in ensuring the reliability and quality of these systems. In this comprehensive exploration, we delve into the intricate components of AI systems, focusing on User Interface and API layers. The journey begins with a meticulous examination of User Interface testing, where manual validation and automated tools are harnessed to ensure adherence to functional standards. Transitioning to the Integration Layer using API Interfaces, we unravel the significance of APIs in AI systems and lay the groundwork for fundamental API testing. Beyond the surface, we explore the probabilistic nature of AI systems, delving into specialized evaluation methods and statistical analyses. The journey concludes by delving into AI-based quality metrics, emphasizing accuracy, precision, and recall, essential benchmarks for Quality Engineers navigating the intricacies of AI-infused applications.

End-to-End Application Testing for User Interface and API Layers

End-to-end testing is essential in evaluating the functionality and reliability of AI systems. It encompasses testing the user interface (UI) to ensure it meets design standards and validating the integration of AI components through APIs. This section delves into the testing strategies for UI and API layers, with a focus on both manual and automated validation methods, as well as the importance of APIs in AI system integration.

User Interface Testing

User interfaces are a key component of AI systems, as they represent the outcomes of AI processes to the end-users via web or mobile applications. Ensuring the functionality and usability of these interfaces is critical to delivering a seamless user experience.

- **Manual Validation**: Manual validation involves testers reviewing the UI manually, verifying that the results match predefined test cases without the use of automated tools. This process ensures that the UI adheres to functional requirements and design standards, providing an effective means to catch any issues that may arise during AI system operation.

- **Automated Validation**: Automated testing tools, such as open-source options like Selenium and Robot Framework, or commercial tools like Tricentis TOSCA and IBM RFT, can execute tasks automatically. These tools compare actual outcomes with expected results, enhancing the efficiency and consistency of UI testing for AI systems. Automation enables faster testing cycles and can handle repetitive validation tasks more effectively.

Integration Layer Testing using API Interfaces

API interfaces serve as the foundation for interaction and integration between various components of AI systems, linking the AI models with external systems or user interfaces.

- **Importance of API Interfaces**: APIs are vital for enabling communication between AI components and other system modules. In AI applications like virtual assistants or chatbots (e.g., Watson Assistant, Azure LUIS), APIs facilitate the exchange of data and requests, exposing AI functionalities to external systems and ensuring seamless integration.

- **Testing Basics for API Interfaces**: API testing involves assessing how different system components — such as AI modules, non-AI modules, and user interfaces — interact with each other. A strong understanding of API testing principles, such as checking for correct data transmission, response times, and error handling, is essential for evaluating the performance of AI systems and ensuring smooth integration across components.

Evaluating the Probabilistic Nature of AI Systems

AI systems are inherently probabilistic, meaning their results may vary depending on factors like training data and environmental conditions. Evaluating such systems requires specialized approaches to account for their uncertainty and variability.

- **Probability-Based Evaluation**: AI applications lack definitive pass/fail outcomes, making probability-based evaluation necessary. This approach involves setting a confidence threshold and assessing the likelihood that AI predictions are accurate. By performing statistical evaluations on multiple data points, testers can measure the system's reliability and accuracy.

- **Statistical Evaluation Metrics**: AI component evaluation includes the use of large datasets to assess performance. Statistical methods help determine the consistency of results, ensuring that an AI system produces reliable predictions when given consistent input data. Previous chapters have elaborated on the importance of consistency and statistical methods in evaluating AI systems.

Test Results Evaluation using AI-Based Metrics

AI applications require specific metrics to assess the performance and accuracy of machine learning models. This section introduces key evaluation metrics and how they are applied in testing AI-infused applications.

- **Key Metrics Overview**: In AI quality engineering, metrics such as accuracy, precision, and recall are essential for evaluating model performance. These metrics provide insights into the model's ability to make correct predictions, as well as its rate of false positives and false negatives.

- **Usage in Evaluation**: Balancing accuracy, precision, and recall is especially critical when dealing with imbalanced datasets. Metrics like the F1 score, which harmonizes precision and recall, help ensure that AI models are evaluated comprehensively. Adjusting decision thresholds and considering domain-specific requirements further enhances the evaluation process.

- **Domain-Specific Considerations**: The choice between precision and recall often depends on the application's context. For example, in medical diagnostics, high recall is typically prioritized to capture all potential cases of a disease, even if it results in more false positives. Understanding these domain-specific trade-offs is crucial for selecting the appropriate metric to guide testing.

Testing AI-infused applications requires a comprehensive approach that incorporates manual and automated validation techniques for both UI and API layers. Given the probabilistic nature of AI systems, specialized evaluation methods, such as probability-based assessments and statistical analyses, are crucial for ensuring the system's reliability. Furthermore, AI-based metrics like accuracy, precision, and recall play a pivotal role in evaluating the performance of machine learning models. Mastery of these testing methodologies and metrics is essential for Quality Engineers to effectively evaluate and enhance the performance of AI-infused applications.

Reporting and Communicating AI-Driven Evaluation Outcomes

Reporting the outcomes of AI-driven evaluations is a crucial part of the delivery lifecycle. It provides essential insights that help assess the quality and performance of AI-infused applications at every phase. This section focuses on the importance of effectively reporting quality engineering (QE) outcomes for AI applications, emphasizing both common practices and specific customizations required for AI systems. The goal is to structure reports in a way that makes the results understandable and actionable.

Quality of Data in AI-Driven Applications

As discussed in previous chapters, the quality of data plays a vital role in training AI systems. The reporting of data quality assessments should reflect the depth of analysis covered earlier, providing detailed insights into the data's role in the AI model's performance. This section outlines the key steps for reporting the outcome of data quality evaluations for AI applications.

Input Data Profile

Profiling the data used to train and test AI-infused applications is essential to understanding the effectiveness of the data. Here are some key aspects to consider:

- **Volumetrics of Data**: This includes the size and scope of the data, such as the number of rows (data points) and columns (features) that influence the prediction of the output. Understanding data volume helps gauge the dataset's capacity to represent real-world scenarios.

- **Type of Data**: Identifying the modalities of the data—whether it's structured data, time series, unstructured text, audio, video, or image data—provides insight into how the AI system processes and interprets different data types.

- **Lexical Diversity**: In AI applications, especially those involving text data, understanding the vocabulary and linguistic variations is essential. Metrics like the presence of abbreviations, accents, contractions, and other text-based elements contribute to the assessment of lexical diversity.

Data Quality Assessment

The assessment of data quality should be based on the metrics discussed in earlier chapters. For instance, in Natural Language Processing (NLP) applications, key metrics to evaluate include:

- **Class Confusion**: Identifying instances where the model confuses one class or category with another, which can affect model accuracy.

- **Semantic Space Representation**: Analyzing how well the input data correlates with output labels and the overall semantic structure of the data.

- **Correlation of Input Data and Output Labels**: Ensuring that there is a strong and meaningful relationship between the data fed into the model and the predicted outcomes.

Documenting Observations

It is essential to document the findings from the data profiling and quality assessment. This documentation serves as a basis for improving the AI model's performance. Key points to document include:

- **Metrics Represented in the Training Data**: Identify which quality metrics are represented in the training data. For example, in a conversational system, lexical diversity might be reflected in the use of abbreviations, accents, or volumetrics.

- **Metrics Not Represented in the Training Data**: Document any metrics that are lacking in the training data. For instance, if contractions or variations in sentence complexity are absent from the training data of a conversational system, this could affect its performance.

- **Interpretation of Data Quality Metrics**: Providing an interpretation of the data quality metrics is crucial for understanding the system's behavior. For example, analyzing which utterances may cause confusion among intents in a conversational system can help refine the model's accuracy.

Recommendations for Improving Data Quality and Testing

Once the data quality assessment is complete, the next step is to provide actionable recommendations for improvement. This could include:

- **Improving Underperforming Data Quality Metrics**: Data quality issues can be addressed by synthesizing new data. For example, if the conversational system lacks contractions in its training data, more data representing such variations can be added to improve its performance.

- **Addressing the Lack of Data Variations**: If the AI system is trained on simplistic or limited data variations, testing should include more diverse data combinations. For instance, if a conversational system is only trained on simple sentence structures, more complex sentence variations should be added to the testing process.

Visualizing Data Metrics

The test report should include the sections mentioned above along with visual representations of the data metrics. Visual aids such as graphs, charts, and tables help to present the data quality assessment in an easily understandable format. The figure below illustrates a sample representation of a data quality metric assessment, providing a clear visual summary of the findings.

By including these structured sections in the report, stakeholders can gain a comprehensive understanding of the data quality and testing insights, facilitating better decision-making for improving the AI system.

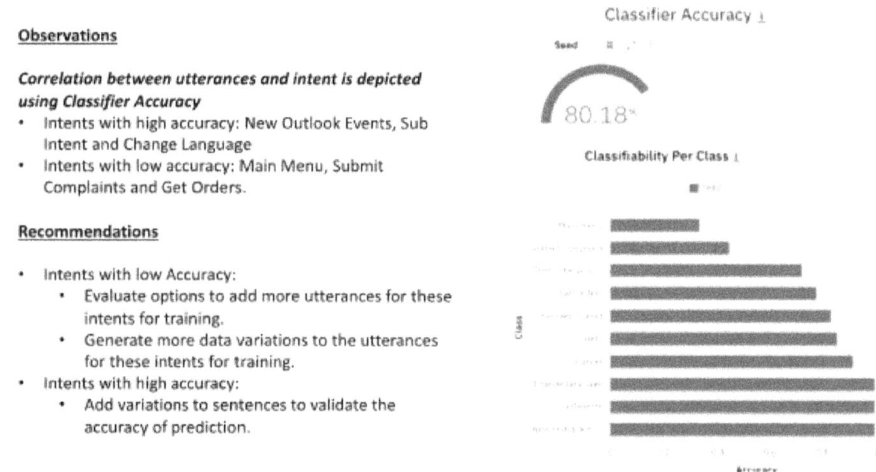

Figure 8.2: Sample Report for Data Quality Metrics

Test Design and Scripting

Test Design and scripting for AI infused applications is very similar to traditional deterministic applications. The key inputs needed to report in test design are:

- Ability to combine Data Insights and functional insights to create test cases.

- Use Model based test design approach. The report should have the test coverage achieved from this approach.

- Test Cases generated from model-based testing approach should be included.

- Test scripting approach using the test automation framework should be included. If Gherkin scripts are used, then they must be presented in the report.

A sample test design report is visualized in Fig. 8.3

Figure 8.3: Sample Test Design Report from a tool

Test Execution

Test Execution report should have inputs like traditional application testing report with some changes. The key inputs needed to report in test execution are:

- Step by Step execution of the test scripts.

- Screenshots of every step executed.

- Stepwise test results: Passed or Failed.

- Test case level test results: Passed, Failed or To Be Statistically Evaluate.

- Test Step and Test Case Execution Time.

Below is a sample test report (Fig. 8.4) from a custom test execution framework:

Automated Test Case Execution

Test Execution

- Automated Test Case Execution
  - API level test execution is performed for large number of data points.
  - User Interface test execution is performed to validate the end-to-end user experience validation.
  - IBM's OTFA (Optimized Test Flow Automation) is developed over Selenium. It also ability to evaluate Partially Passed (To Be Statistically Evaluate) test cases as well.
  - TOSCA supports the test case automation at API and UI level.
- Provided ability to run tests on local browser, server unattended mode on different platforms and multiple browsers. Can be integrated with Jenkins pipeline

- Test Reports – Step by step results and screen shots provided.

- Ability to Record test scenarios – Perform user actions, record and import into Test execution and create it as a test case

- Ability to capture dynamic elements and validate

Figure 8.4: A sample test execution report

AI Model Evaluation

AI model evaluation report should have the sensitivity assessment and adversarial robustness evaluation report.

- Sensitivity assessment capabilities should be included.
- Test data generated for each of the capability should be provided.
- Test execution outcome for each of the test data for every capability.
- Consolidated statistical report for each capability.
- Interpretation of the statistical output.

A sample output report for AI model evaluation from a custom solution is given below (Fig.8.5):

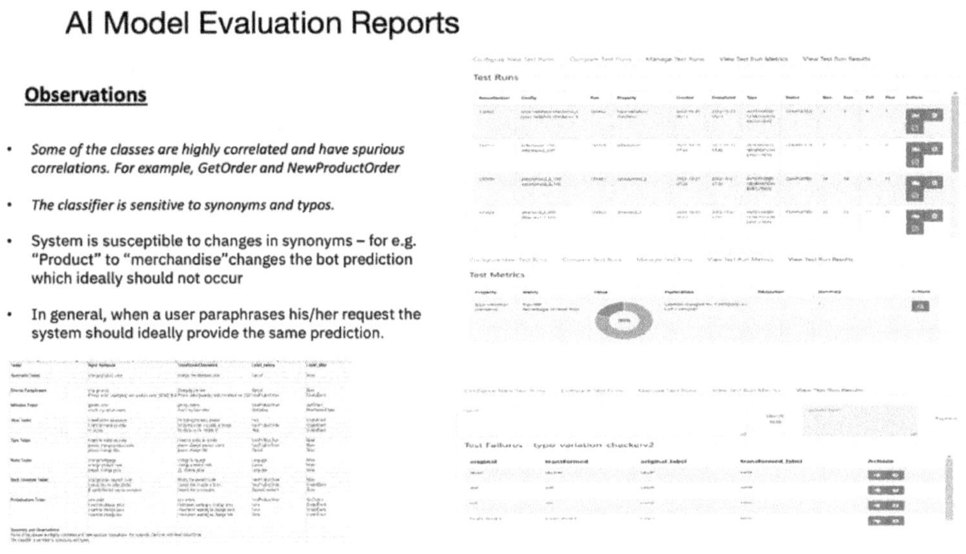

AI Model Evaluation Reports

Figure 8.5: A Sample AI Model Evaluation Report

Effectively reporting on quality engineering practices for AI-based solutions is crucial for developing reliable and robust applications. By focusing on data quality, test design, execution, and AI model evaluation, aspiring quality engineers can play a key role in the successful development and deployment of AI-infused applications. Continuously refining reporting processes based on insights gained from testing experiences will drive ongoing improvement and excellence in quality engineering for AI.

Best Practices for AI Testing

In the rapidly evolving field of artificial intelligence (AI), ensuring the quality and reliability of AI-driven systems is critical. Quality Engineers play a pivotal role in overcoming the unique challenges that come with the probabilistic nature of AI components. This guide outlines best practices specifically designed for new Quality Engineers tasked with evaluating the quality of AI-based systems. The sections below focus on key challenges such as data quality dependency, the absence of predicted outcomes (ground truth), non-binary representations, test coverage issues, and evaluation using statistical accuracy. By following these practices, Quality Engineers can make a significant contribution to developing robust and ethically sound AI applications, while adapting their testing strategies to the ever-advancing landscape of AI technology.

Dependency on Data Quality

Data quality is foundational to AI testing. As AI systems rely heavily on data to make predictions and decisions, ensuring high-quality data is essential to achieving reliable outcomes.

Data Quality Assessment

The following points are in consideration:

- Conduct thorough analyses of the training data to identify and address potential issues.
- Implement data cleaning techniques to correct incomplete, inconsistent, duplicate, or biased data.
- Utilize statistical methods to assess the overall quality of the dataset.

Diversity in Data Sources

The following points are in consideration:

- Collect data from varied sources to ensure a comprehensive representation of real-world scenarios.
- Incorporate both structured and unstructured data to improve the model's ability to handle diverse input formats.
- Implement strategies to balance the representation of different data combinations.

Bias Detection and Mitigation

The following points are in consideration:

- Regularly monitor and identify biases in the training dataset.
- Use techniques like oversampling underrepresented data and applying debiasing methods to mitigate bias.
- Incorporate ethical considerations during data collection to ensure fairness.

Absence of Predicted Outcomes (Ground Truth)

AI systems often face challenges due to the absence of predefined outcomes, especially in unsupervised machine learning. Developing a flexible evaluation framework is crucial in these scenarios.

Dynamic Evaluation Framework

The following points are in consideration:

- Create an evaluation framework that can adapt to the dynamic outcomes of unsupervised learning models.
- Set benchmarks based on clustering performance or feature extraction.
- Use metrics like silhouette score and Davies-Bouldin index to quantify the effectiveness of data segmentation.

Continuous Monitoring

The following points are in consideration:

- Implement continuous monitoring of model outcomes to track performance over time.
- Establish feedback loops to adjust evaluation criteria based on observed changes in model behavior.
- Use anomaly detection to flag unexpected shifts in outcomes.

Outcomes Not Represented in Binary Format

Many AI systems produce results that are probabilistic in nature, making it necessary to establish processes for interpreting and acting on these outcomes.

Confidence Score Analysis

The following points are in consideration:

- Develop systematic methods for interpreting and using confidence scores.
- Set threshold values for confidence scores tailored to specific use cases.
- Adjust confidence scores dynamically based on real-world performance and feedback.

User-Focused Communication

The following points are in consideration:

- Design user interfaces that clearly convey probabilistic outcomes to users.
- Provide clear explanations of confidence scores and what they mean.
- Solicit user feedback to enhance the transparency and interpretability of

the system's outputs.

Test Coverage Challenges

Ensuring comprehensive test coverage is essential for validating AI systems, especially given their inherent variability and complexity.

Iterative Testing Approach

The following points are in consideration:

- Adopt an iterative testing approach to accommodate the evolving nature of AI systems.

- Use cross-validation techniques to assess model performance across different datasets.

- Regularly update test scenarios based on emerging patterns and user feedback.

Comprehensive Data Coverage

The following points are in consideration:

- Increase the diversity of test data to cover a wide range of user inputs and scenarios.

- Regularly review test coverage against new data patterns.

- Use adaptive testing strategies to prioritize new and changing test scenarios.

Evaluation Using Statistical Accuracy

Statistical accuracy is a cornerstone of AI testing, but it must be integrated with other evaluation techniques to provide a full picture of the system's performance.

Functional Testing Incorporation

The following points are in consideration:

- Extend traditional accuracy assessments to include functional testing.

- Simulate real-world conditions to evaluate the system's performance in practical scenarios.

- Use user-centered testing methods to capture insights not reflected in traditional statistical accuracy measures.

User Feedback Integration

The following points are in consideration:

- Actively seek user feedback to validate system accuracy in real-world contexts.
- Refine statistical models using user input to improve performance.
- Balance user satisfaction metrics with traditional accuracy measures.

Probabilistic Nature of AI Components

AI systems often generate probabilistic results, requiring specific evaluation methods to ensure system reliability and robustness.

Understanding Probabilistic Outputs

The following points are in consideration:

- Recognize that AI or machine learning systems produce probabilistic outcomes, not definitive pass/fail results.
- Accept that AI results come with associated confidence scores that indicate the reliability of predictions.

Threshold Confidence Score Setting

The following points are in consideration:

- Set a threshold confidence score (e.g., 75%) as a benchmark for accepting outputs.
- Outputs that exceed the threshold are accepted without further scrutiny, while those below the threshold undergo additional testing.

Statistical Evaluation for Low Confidence

The following points are in consideration:

- Conduct statistical evaluations for results falling below the established confidence threshold.
- Re-test using different data points to validate predictions statistically.
- Use metrics such as accuracy, precision, and recall assessing low-confidence outcomes.

Testing AI Components with Large Datasets and APIs

AI systems often need to process large datasets or interact with APIs, making testing these components critical for scalability and reliability.

API Layer Testing

The following points are in consideration:

- Test the API layer with large datasets to ensure cost-effective and efficient testing.
- After unit testing, focus on API testing during system integration or functional testing phases to assess scalability.

Consistency Testing

The following points are in consideration:

- Test for consistency by verifying that outputs remain consistent when the input data is stable.
- Identify any inconsistencies in predicted outcomes, which may suggest issues with AI or machine learning components.

End-to-End Testing Automation

The following points are in consideration:

- Automate end-to-end testing processes wherever possible to improve efficiency.
- Integrate automated testing into the DevOps pipeline for continuous and unattended testing.

Ensuring Regulatory Compliance in AI-Driven Solutions

It is critical for AI solutions to comply with various regulations to ensure ethical and legal standards are met.

Legal Compliance

The following points are in consideration:

- Comply with data protection and privacy laws like GDPR.
- Prevent bias and discrimination, adhering to anti-discrimination regulations.

- Follow intellectual property and cybersecurity laws and ensure contractual obligations are met.

Ethical Compliance

The following points are in consideration:

- Address biases and promote fairness in AI systems.
- Ensure transparency in decision-making processes.
- Set up accountability mechanisms and ethical guidelines and maintain human oversight.

Engagement and Alignment

The following points are in consideration:

- Engage with stakeholders and the public to incorporate diverse perspectives.
- Align with international standards and guidelines to ensure ethical AI deployment.
- Continuously adapt to evolving AI ethics and regulations.

Test Reporting for AI-Based Solutions: A Comprehensive Guide

Effective test reporting is essential for tracking the quality of AI systems. This section outlines the critical components for creating comprehensive test reports.

Data Quality Assessment Report

The following points are in consideration:

- Thoroughly evaluate the data used for AI training and testing.
- Use key metrics (e.g., NLP analytics) for robust data quality assessment.
- Document insights from data profiling and quality assessments.
- Identify and recommend strategies for enhancing data quality.

Test Execution Report

The following points are in consideration:

- Develop detailed test execution reports for AI applications.
- Include step-by-step execution details, along with test results (passed/

failed).

- Capture screenshots for every executed step and document execution times.

AI Model Evaluation Report

The following points are in consideration:

- Assess sensitivity capabilities of the AI model.
- Document test data for each capability and corresponding test execution outcomes.
- Provide consolidated statistical reports and interpret statistical output.

Mastering best practices for AI testing is vital for ensuring the quality and reliability of AI-driven applications. By implementing these strategies, Quality Engineers can have a substantial impact on the success of AI projects, promoting continuous improvements and innovation. As AI technology advances, testing strategies should evolve accordingly to address new challenges, ensuring that AI applications remain robust, ethically sound, and compliant with regulations.

Conclusion

In this chapter, we have gone through a comprehensive approach to AI quality engineering, emphasizing the importance of data quality, robust test design, and effective evaluation of AI models. We explored the challenges of testing probabilistic AI systems and highlighted best practices for ensuring reliability, consistency, and ethical soundness. The chapter also stressed the need for continuous improvement and adaptability in testing methodologies, equipping Quality Engineers with the tools and insights necessary for navigating the complexities of AI applications. Looking ahead, we will delve into essential knowledge, career opportunities, and ongoing learning in AI Quality Assurance.

Exercise: Test Your Understanding

Answer the following questions and test your understanding of learning from Chapter 8:

Q. 1. What is a crucial consideration in AI applications when assessing data quality?

- A. Quantity of data
- B. Consistency of data
- X. Data variety
- Δ. Data Confidentiality

Q. 2. Which approach, exemplified by Combinatorial Test Design (CTD), uses mathematical models to identify points of variation for generating test scenarios?

    A. Random testing

    B. Model-driven testing

    C. Scenario-based testing

    D. Behavior-driven development (BDD)

Q. 3. What is a crucial aspect to ensure in AI model outputs for consistent and reliable performance?

    A. Inconsistency in results

    B. High sensitivity

    C. Dynamic threshold setting to evaluate the confidence score

    D. Variability in statistical outcomes

Q. 4. Why are API interfaces integral to AI systems?

    A. To improve data quality

    B. To expose AI components for interaction and integration

    C. To enhance user interface design

    D. To reduce test design complexity

Q. 5. What should be documented in the Data Quality Assessment Report?

    A. List of test cases

    B. Recommendations for improving data quality

    C. Execution time of test scripts

    D. API interface details

Appendix-A
Answers - Test your understanding

CHAPTER 1

Answers to test your understanding, Chapter 1

Ans.1. B
Ans.2. C
Ans.3. B
Ans.4. D
Ans.5. C

CHAPTER 2

Answers to test your understanding, Chapter 2

Ans.1. A
Ans.2. B
Ans.3. C
Ans.4. A
Ans.5. A and C

CHAPTER 3

Answers to test your understanding, Chapter 3

Ans.1. C
Ans.2. C
Ans.3. C
Ans.4. A
Ans.5. A

CHAPTER 4

Answers to test your understanding, Chapter 4

Ans.1. C
Ans.2. A
Ans.3. B
Ans.4. C
Ans.5. C

CHAPTER 5

Answers to test your understanding, Chapter 5

Ans.1. B
Ans.2. C
Ans.3. C
Ans.4. A
Ans.5. B

CHAPTER 6

Answers to test your understanding, Chapter 6

Ans.1. B
Ans.2. B
Ans.3. C
Ans.4. A
Ans.5. B.

CHAPTER 7

Answers to test your understanding, Chapter 7

Ans.1. C
Ans.2. A
Ans.3. C
Ans.4. C
Ans.5. C

CHAPTER 8

Answers to test your understanding, Chapter 8

Ans.1. B
Ans.2. B
Ans.3. C
Ans.4. B
Ans.5. B

Appendix-B
Learning Opportunities

In the rapidly evolving realm of Artificial Intelligence (AI), Generative AI (GenAI) and Quality Engineering (QE), the pursuit of expertise demands a multifaceted blend of specialized skills, continual learning, and a growth-oriented mindset. This chapter navigates through fundamental knowledge, educational resources, certifications, and professional development opportunities imperative for aspiring AI QE specialists. This chapter highlights the integration of Generative AI into all Quality Engineering (QE) job roles, rather than focusing on a specific career path for AI or Generative AI.

To gain a solid understanding of Artificial Intelligence (AI) and Machine Learning (ML), it's essential to explore both foundational and advanced topics. The following resources include courses and books that cover the basics of AI, ML principles, and specialized areas like generative models and natural language processing (NLP). These materials are perfect for anyone looking to enhance their knowledge and expertise in these rapidly evolving fields.

Books

The followings are the books can be considered:
- Harness AI's Creative Power to Drive Innovation
- Prompt Engineering for Beginners: A Comprehensive Guide
- Embracing the Power of Cloud Hosting for Banking Solutions
- Agile Odyssey: Unlock Your Inner Leader, Inspire Transformation, and Drive Success

Certifications

The followings are the most popular certifications in Quality Engineering:

- ISTQB Certified Tester AI Testing (CT-AI): International certification that validates your understanding of AI testing principles and practices, with a focus on AI-based systems and deep learning applications.

- AI-Related Certifications: Additional syllabi from A4Q, AiU, and CSTQB/KSTQB are recommended by ISTQB.

- Microsoft Certified Azure AI Fundamentals: Introduction to Azure AI services and tools relevant for GenAI QE specialists.

- Google Cloud AI Platform Specialization: Expertise in building, deploying, and managing AI models on Google Cloud.

- OpenAI API Certification: Learn to utilize OpenAI's API to develop and test AI applications.

Training Programs

The followings are the competitive Training Programs; go through each program's official web site before you opt:

- DeepLearning.AI Professional Certificate: Comprehensive training in deep learning theory and practice.

- Fast.ai's Practical Deep Learning for Coders: Combines lectures with hands-on coding projects for deep learning skills.

- OpenAI API Developer Course: Offers hands-on experience with OpenAI's API for building and deploying AI applications.

- GenAI QE Bootcamps: Intensive programs that equip participants with specific GenAI QE skills.

Appendix-C
Summarizing the key takeaways from the book

This comprehensive resource explores the intricate realm of Quality Engineering Methods for AI-driven solutions. It addresses critical aspects such as data quality, the nuances of model-based test design, strategies for continuous improvement, and the transformative impact of Generative AI. Each chapter provides invaluable insights for Quality Engineers navigating the dynamic field of artificial intelligence.

More than just a collection of chapters, this resource serves as a thorough guide that tackles key challenges, presents practical solutions, and promotes best practices essential for success in AI testing methodologies. From analyzing AI system components to understanding AI-specific quality metrics and considering the ethical implications of Generative AI, this guide equips professionals with the knowledge and tools required for effective quality engineering. As technology continues to evolve, this resource stands as a testament to the adaptability and excellence demanded in the ever-changing landscape of AI testing.

To gain a solid understanding of Artificial Intelligence (AI) and Machine Learning (ML), it's essential to explore both foundational and advanced topics. The following resources include courses and books that cover the basics of AI, ML principles, and specialized areas like generative models and natural language processing (NLP). These materials are perfect for anyone looking to enhance their knowledge and expertise in these rapidly evolving fields.

Outlining a framework for quality engineers to become Technical Experts in AI testing

Becoming a Technical Expert in AI testing is a journey that demands acquiring specific skills, gaining valuable experience, demonstrating leadership qualities, fostering innovation, and building eminence. This framework provides a comprehensive guide for Quality Engineers aspiring to excel in AI testing.

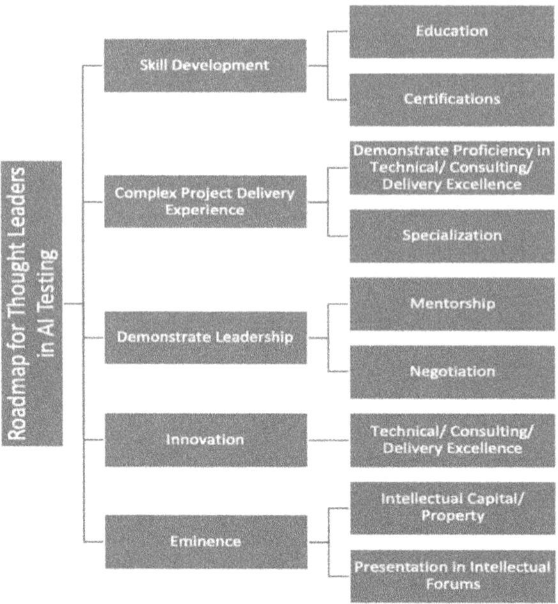

Figure C.1: Framework to Technical Expertise in AI Testing

To establish yourself as a Technical Expert in AI testing, it's essential to continuously develop your skills and knowledge in this field.

As Quality Engineers aspiring to become Technical Experts, the knowledge in this book provides a solid foundation for your transformation. Drawing from their extensive experience, the authors share invaluable insights and lessons learned, offering a framework for navigating the dynamic landscape of AI testing. Becoming a Technical Expert in AI testing involves more than mastering tools or methodologies; it requires a holistic evolution encompassing technical expertise, strategic thinking, and effective collaboration. This book has carefully guided you through understanding AI fundamentals, assessing probabilistic systems, tailoring quality engineering practices, employing AI to enhance QE, and exploring the transformative potential of generative AI. Each chapter builds your skillset and knowledge, preparing you to influence the future of AI testing. The authors' real-world experiences emphasize the importance of tailoring solutions to client challenges, clarifying roles within interdisciplinary teams, and focusing on capabilities over tool evaluation. These insights serve as guiding principles, encouraging adaptability, teamwork, and a client-focused approach. As you advance toward becoming a Technical Expert, heed the authors' advice to prioritize capabilities, engage stakeholders early, and conduct in-depth interviews to gain deeper understanding. Building a successful career in AI testing requires fostering expertise through continuous learning, recognizing market needs, identifying key stakeholders, and maintaining regular communication with clients. Remember, the journey to Technical

Expertise is not a sprint but an ongoing process of growth and discovery. Embrace opportunities to contribute to the AI testing community, develop your personal brand, and stay informed about emerging trends. The framework provided in this book extends beyond its pages, inspiring you to carve your unique path and leave a lasting impact in the ever-evolving field of AI testing. May this book ignite your ascent to Technical Expertise, where your innovation, dedication, and expertise redefine the future of quality engineering in the AI era. Your journey has just begun—embrace it with enthusiasm, curiosity, and an unwavering commitment to excellence. Best of luck on this thrilling and rewarding path ahead!

In conclusion, the following are the main points that outline the framework:

- Foundation of Knowledge
- Skill Development
- Practical Application
- Continuous Learning and Adaptation
- Building Expertise
- Long-Term Vision
- Key Success Practices

JOIN US ON THE
ARCCHIE PUBLICATIONS
DISCORD SERVER

Connect with fellow readers, authors, and enthusiasts to discuss all things related to our publications and the exciting world of AI, programming, and learning. Share your insights, ask questions, and engage in vibrant discussions to expand your knowledge and inspire creativity. Take advantage of this opportunity to be part of a dynamic community dedicated to exploring the frontiers of technology and innovation. Join our Discord Server today and be part of the ARCCHIE Publications community!

https://discord.gg/z26SenmpEt